## CONVERSATION BETWEEN GOD AND MAN

The author, Dr. G. Venkataraman, is a Physicist by profession, served first at the Bhabha Atomic Research Centre, Mumbai [1955-1973], and then at the Indira Gandhi Centre for Atomic Research, Kalpakkam [1973-1987]. Later, he set up and became the first Director of ANURAG [a unit of Defence Research and Development Organisation - DRDO], which was established for chip design and the design of parallel super computers. A Jawarharlal Nehru Fellow and a Fellow of several science academies, he has written many books on Physics, including a major scientific biography of Sir C.V. Raman. Attracted by the Spiritual teachings of Bhagavan Baba, he came in 1992 [after retirement] to Puttaparthi, where he has been ever since, teaching at the Sri Sathya Sai University. For one term, he also served as the Vice Chancellor of that University.

# CONVERSATION BETWEEN
# GOD AND MAN

G. Venkataraman

A Sai Blossom product of
The Media Division of
THE SRI SATHYA SAI SADHANA TRUST

**THE MEDIA DIVISION**
**SRI SATHYA SAI SADHANA TRUST**

*Registered Office*
Prashanti Nilayam, 515 134,
Anantapur District, Andhra Pradesh
INDIA


First published 2009

ISBN-978-81-908439-0-4

*Page and Cover design*
Prasanna, Krishna and Ajish

*Printed at*

Seshaasai e-Forms (P) Ltd.
Mumbai

*Published by*

The Media Division
Sri Sathya Sai Sadhana Trust
Prashanti Nilayam, 515 134
Anantapur District, A.P
India

# *Contents*

# PREFACE

The *Srimad Bhagavad Gita* is more than five thousand years old, being a record of an immortal conversation between God and man. Old the *Gita* might be in terms of passage of time; yet it has survived, having been published a countless number of times, and translated into hundreds of languages. It has also been extensively commented upon and written about for centuries, while in recent times, there have also been many films as well as television serials. You might therefore wonder whether one more book on the *Gita* is at all required, and if so, what is new or different about this book.

There are indeed a few important differences where this book is concerned. The first is that the *Gita* is presented as a **SIMPLE** conversation between God and man, and in the language of the day. It is almost like the conversation we might have with God freely raising our doubts and so on, if He were to appear before us. Many might wonder whether taking such a liberty would not diminish the sanctity of the original *Gita*, held in great reverence by millions for thousands of years; there is some merit in such an argument. However, after listening to countless discourses of Bhagavan Sri Sathya Sai Baba, I have come to the conclusion that the **ESSENCE** of the *Gita* is **more important to humanity today than ever before in human history.** As a result, I strongly believe that every effort must be made to get across that message in as simple and effective a manner as possible, which is why I have taken a huge liberty in presenting the *Gita* the way I have done; I sincerely hope that the result is worth the risk I have taken.

The *Gita* is not, as is commonly imagined, merely about Krishna giving advice to Arjuna to shed his doubts and get on with the fight. Nor is it specific to any particular religion or school of Spiritual philosophy, as many seem to believe. Rather, it is all about a **LIFE BOAT,** which, if availed of, can save individuals, entire communities and indeed the whole of humanity, from being drowned by the innumerable difficulties that plague today's Society at the macro as well as the micro level.

To some, this might appear like a tall claim; however, I request you to suspend your disbelief until you have gone through the book thoroughly, and also read the detailed reflections I offer at the end, after the dialogue between Krishna and Arjuna comes to a close. You would then appreciate [I hope!] how the Message of the *Gita* is Universal, Timeless, and exactly what we need to tackle the huge and massive problems humanity faces today, all the way from global terrorism to climate change, with many other complex issues thrown in between. Hopefully, you would also get some idea of how, over the ages, saints, seers and noble souls in all lands, each in their own particular way, have intuitively cognised the Divine Nature of the Individual Soul and given expression to it via Love and Compassion, bringing cheer to the miserable and hope to those feeling abandoned. If, as Sage Aurobindo once dreamt, the Pure Love that resides in every Heart can get connected, and humanity as a whole rises in a huge Tsunami of Pure Love, all our problems would, without any doubt, get swept away! It is to bring home this crucial fact that I have adopted a novel approach in preparing and offering this book.

A few words now about how the *Gita* actually came to be taught to Arjuna on the eve of the epic war fought thousands of years ago in the battlefield in Kurukshetra, between the Kauravas and Pandavas. Briefly, the facts are as follows:

The starting point of it all was the greed and jealousy of the Kauravas, which led them to trick the Pandavas, grab their kingdom, and banish the latter to fourteen years of exile; the understanding was that at the end of the exile period, the kingdom would be returned to the Pandavas. However, the Kauravas did not honour their promise. War then seemed inevitable, and Krishna went as an emissary to the court of the Kauravas to work out a peace deal; that attempt failed.

It was time for war, and both Pandavas as well as Kauravas sought help from Krishna. Krishna offered the two parties a choice: Either His armies or Himself, but only as an advisor. The Kauravas opted for the armies, while Arjuna who went to Krishna on behalf of the Pandavas sought only Krishna, even though Krishna would not bear arms. Thus it was that Krishna became the Charioteer of Arjuna.

In accordance with the tradition of those days, the rules of war were drafted and adopted by both sides. The battle was to be fought in an open space in a place called Kurukshetra, not far from where both the Pandavas and the Kauravas lived. A day for the commencement of the war was also fixed.

That day finally arrived and the two armies assembled in full formation on the battlefield. They all were there, the foot soldiers, the elephants, the horses, and the principal warriors in their respective chariots. Arjuna too was present, with Krishna, God in human form, driving his chariot. The two opposing sides were supposed to be enemies, ready to fight a bloody war to settle a dispute. And yet, in keeping with noble traditions unique to India (or Bharat), Yudhishtra, the eldest among the Pandavas, gets down from his chariot and walks over to the side of the Kauravas, to offer his respects to his grandfather, Bhishma, and other elders especially his *Gurus*, Kripacharya and Dronacharya. Taking the lead from their elder brother, ever the stickler for adherence to *Dharma*, the other Pandavas, too do the same. Everyone assembled on the battlefield is stunned, while some are deeply touched.

Respects offered, the Pandavas return to their formation and take their respective places. Everyone then blows his conch, as a signal that he is ready. Arjuna and Krishna too do the same. At that moment, for some unknown reason [was it really unknown or ordained by the Lord?] Arjuna asks Krishna to drive the chariot to the as yet empty "no-man's land" in the middle, so that he could survey both sides. Krishna does so, and the stage is now set for God in human form to do what He had really incarnated for–to teach mankind *Atma Vidya* or the Knowledge of the Self. It is this Knowledge that is enshrined in the *Gita*.

For well over half a century, Bhagavan Sri Sathya Sai Baba has been living the very essence of the *Gita*, reminding us via not only His innumerable teachings but also His many acts of great compassion, how the *Gita* is an Eternal "survival kit" for everyone, and for all times. Further, through innumerable Discourses delivered over decades, Baba has brought to light many subtle nuances not well understood before; more importantly, He has explained the essence in such a manner that one can relate the lessons of the *Gita* to today's life. Most important of all, by drawing attention to the Cosmic relationship between humans and Creation, Baba has given mankind an amazing roadmap for solving the complex problems of today, ranging from terrorism to climate change. Sounds unbelievable? Please read on and find out for yourself!

With much love, deep humility and enormous reverence, I dedicate this book to Bhagavan Baba, but for Whom, I would have continued to remain in total ignorance of the Supreme Teaching of the Lord.

Chapter 1

# THE FOG OF DOUBT SETS IN

**The day of the battle finally arrives, and the two opposing armies assemble on the battlefield in full formation, the Kauravas on one side and the Pandavas on the other. As per the previous arrangement, Krishna is on the side of the Pandavas, unarmed of course. Instead of participating in the fighting, He is playing the role of a Charioteer; no doubt, it is all a part of an elaborate Divine Drama, the most important aspect of which is just about to unfold.**

**There are still some moments left before the fighting actually starts, and Arjuna asks Krishna to take the chariot to the middle of the theatre of war so that he could simultaneously see both armies in full formation. Krishna does exactly that and once the chariot is in the middle, Arjuna slowly lets his eyes wander.**

**On one side he sees his own army, made up of his brothers, friends, relatives, etc. Likewise, on the other side, Arjuna sees the army of his opponents that includes his cousins, uncles, and various relatives. Towering above them all is his dear grandfather, Bhishma; he also spots his *Gurus*.**

**For the first time, Arjuna is beginning to have doubts. Earlier he was itching to fight and could**

**not wait for the war to start, but now, even as the battle is actually about to commence, He begins to wonder whether war is such a good idea and really worth it, given the devastation that combats always cause.**

**Arjuna is in deep distress, and turns to Krishna with his doubts, seeking an answer; and that is where the *Gita* really begins. The inner significance is that when man surrenders to the Lord and seeks help, God is only too happy to come to the rescue.**

**That in brief is how the immortal conversation between Arjuna and Krishna began. It started like a small consultation and a pep talk but soon became not only Krishna's teaching to Arjuna, but an Eternal and Immortal lesson from God to man.**

**Over now to the most important conversation in the history of mankind, that took place on a fateful morning over five thousand years ago, on the battlefield in Kurukshetra.**

ARJUNA: Krishna, looking at the two armies in full readiness and the fighting just about to start, I must confess that I am beginning to have doubts and am not sure if I can fight in this war.

KRISHNA: Arjuna, what has happened to you suddenly? Why are you talking like this?

ARJUNA: You want to know Krishna? Let me tell You.

Bhishma over there is my grandfather! How can I shoot arrows at my own grandfather who has showered so much love on me?

And over there is Dronacharya. He is my *Guru,* Krishna, he is my *Guru!* How can one kill one's own *Guru?* Can there be a greater sin?

KRISHNA: Arjuna, I am really surprised by what you are saying. All along, you were itching for war, and now, all of a sudden, you want to drop out! How come you have become so remorseful at the very last minute? You **can't** quit now; it is too late for that! If you do that, people would call you a coward.

Arjuna, you have **GOT** to cast aside your doubts and misgivings. Get up, and enter into battle!

ARJUNA: Frankly Krishna, I cannot see any great purpose in this war. I am very confused at present. To fight or not to fight–that is my question!

Krishna, I seek refuge in You. Totally surrendering to You, I pray to You for guidance.

**God melts when anyone surrenders to Him. Krishna understands that Arjuna is having a serious problem and decides to help him with some straight talk, imparting Eternal Wisdom at the same time.**

KRISHNA: Arjuna, you are acting like a perfect fool! You are mourning the death of your relatives and friends, even before they have died!

Do you know anything about life, death, and what happens after death? You obviously do not, for if you did, you would not be chickening out like you are trying to do right now.

ARJUNA: Krishna, please try to understand my problem! It is not a trivial one.

KRISHNA: Arjuna, your big problem is that like everyone else, you think you are the body—that is your real problem! You are so used to seeing bodies being born and die. All those images of death have got stuck in your Mind, and that is why you are now worrying about death.

ARJUNA: Krishna! What are all these strange things You are saying? I don't understand a single word!!

KRISHNA: Arjuna, listen to this carefully. Neither you nor I are the body, though we both possess them. I wear My body like a dress and so do you.

Who is this "I" that is wearing the body? Arjuna, it is the Immortal and Universal Soul or the *Atma* that is wearing the body! By the way, there is no such thing as My *Atma*, your *Atma* and so on. It is the same *Atma* that is present everywhere, wearing many dresses. There is only one *Atma*, period.

ARJUNA: Krishna, please! I am totally lost. Here I am,

asking You about the futility of killing my kith and kin, and You are telling me that there is only one *Atma* which is present in all bodies. This is just too much for me! What is this *Atma* You are talking about?

KRISHNA: I can understand your difficulty Arjuna, and maybe an example would make things a bit clearer. Just look up in the sky during the daytime. You will see some clouds here and there, and empty sky in between. Everywhere, including in the spaces between clouds, there is water vapour. In some places, this water vapour manifests as clouds, but elsewhere it is not visible; however, it is present all the same, everywhere and at all times.

Now notice a few interesting points. Firstly, the clouds appear and disappear; they are transient and not permanent. Next, while they exist, the clouds keep changing their shapes. And thirdly, no two clouds are alike.

ARJUNA: Clouds, Krishna? What have they got to do with war? What have they got to do with my specific problem of killing my grandfather and *Gurus*, just for the sake of a kingdom? I am totally lost!

KRISHNA: Patience Arjuna! In due course, you will understand everything, including why I am urging you not to quit.

Let us get back to the clouds. What I want to

point out is that what happens with clouds happens also in the world. The *Atma* pervades the entire world, indeed the entire Universe. Here and there, it manifests temporarily via the "dresses" called bodies, not only of humans but also of animals, insects, etc. Thus, all living beings are the embodiments of the one Universal *Atma*.

Recall what I told you about clouds changing their shapes with time. The same thing happens to a living being or the embodied *Atma*. The being passes through various stages such as childhood, youth, middle age, and old age.

When the body becomes old, the *Atma* just casts off the body and wears a new "dress", that is, it acquires a new body!

Arjuna, there is no need to feel sad because death is just a change of dress, that is all!

ARJUNA: Krishna, all this is so new to me! I need to think a little about this.

KRISHNA: Your problem is that like all humans you are totally focussed on the body. You keep on thinking you are the body, and by doing so, you become attached to the body. This is called *dehabhimaanam* or body-consciousness, and most problems that humans face arise precisely from this body-consciousness.

Tell me Arjuna, are you that dress you are

wearing? No, that is just your dress. You are **not** the dress but **different** from the dress.

In the same way, neither you nor I, or for that matter anyone else, is the body. The *Atma* is our Real Nature.

ARJUNA: Krishna, if everything is the *Atma*, then why is it that people become so sad when someone dies?

**Notice the remarkable and amazing manner in which Krishna very quickly and seamlessly shifts the focus from the transient to the Eternal, namely the *Atma*. Throughout the dialogue, this is something we should always be looking for, namely, how to deal with the present, but tuned always to the Eternal, that is, God.**

CHAPTER 2

# THE REAL PURPOSE OF LIFE

**In the last Chapter, Krishna gave a jolt by dramatically shifting the focus from the transient body to the Eternal *Atma*. He now comes back to earth so to say, by connecting the Purpose of Life with the *Atma*. This point is important because most of humanity today is blissfully unaware of the fact that God has given us life in the human form with a specific purpose.**

KRISHNA: Arjuna, you asked me why people become sad when death occurs. I shall tell you.

Death makes people sad because they foolishly identify themselves with their body; besides, they develop attachment to many other bodies as well; which is why they become upset when the body of a loved one is gone or about to go.

Arjuna, just think. You are a warrior and you have fought in many battles before. Sometimes, you have even slain people in those battles; yet, you were never bothered then. However, today you are feeling miserable even before you have taken the bow in your hand. Why Arjuna, why?

ARJUNA: I really don't know.

KRISHNA: I shall tell you. The answer is simple; you are

feeling miserable today because the people likely to die in this war are **YOURS**. It is this feeling of "mine" that is really troubling you, and not death *per se*.

ARJUNA: Krishna, I am sorry but I am just not able to understand You.

KRISHNA: It is simple Arjuna; do you cry every time a person dies? However, everyone cries when someone near and dear dies. It is all due to this feeling of "mine" that I just mentioned.

ARJUNA: Why exactly does this feeling of "mine" arise?

KRISHNA: It arises because of body-consciousness or a feeling of attachment to the body. You think you are the perishable body and become attached to it. But the truth is that you are **NOT** the transient body but the Eternal *Atma!*

ARJUNA: I am totally lost! Please tell me something more about the *Atma*; maybe that would help.

KRISHNA: Sure, Arjuna, I definitely shall.

The *Atma* is Eternal and **BEYOND** both Space and Time. It is neither born nor does it die. Do you understand that Arjuna? Drona and Bhishma are all embodiments of the *Atma*, just like you and I are. So, how can they die? It is their bodies that would get destroyed, like a dress getting worn out.

Why feel miserable about something trivial like

that? One day or the other, the old dress has to be thrown away. Do you cry when you have to throw away your old dress?

Your problem is that you are focussing on bodies called Drona, Bhishma, etc., rather than the *Atma* embedded within those bodies. Your focus is wrong and that really is your problem!

ARJUNA: Krishna, please pardon me! I just do not see the purpose of all this talk about the *Atma*. I understand that the *Atma* might be important in a Spiritual context. But here we are talking about war, about killing.

I am telling you that I do not want to kill my grandfather, *Gurus*, and blood relatives. It is as simple as that. Why are You complicating matters by telling me things I hardly understand?

KRISHNA: Arjuna, are you suggesting I do not know anything about war and peace? Or about killing and death? Let me explain why I am telling you something about the *Atma*.

You see Arjuna, life is all about actions. There is no moment when we do not act.

ARJUNA: Krishna, are You saying that we act even while sleeping?

KRISHNA: Of course we do. You may be sleeping but does not your heart beat? Do not your lungs breathe? Does not the beating of the heart and breathing by lungs constitute action?

ARJUNA: Alright, there is always some action going on but what has that got to do with the *Atma*?

KRISHNA: Ah, that is where lies the secret of life!

ARJUNA: Krishna, this seems to be the day for riddles! Here we are in the battlefield and I have an important decision to make, while You are playing with me, posing riddles!

KRISHNA: Arjuna, you mistake Me. It is a pity you do not understand how serious I am. I am telling you all this out of compassion for you and because you are My dear friend.

ARJUNA: Krishna, I am sorry I got You wrong. I know You always have my best interest in Your Heart. Forgive me please, and go ahead with what You were saying.

KRISHNA: Good. You see Arjuna, there are a few things you **must** know, the first of which is that all actions in life must be made Spiritual.

ARJUNA: Krishna, Krishna, hold on for a minute please! You say that all actions must be Spiritual. Can war ever be Spiritual?

KRISHNA: Arjuna! Why do you have to be so impatient? Just hear me out, will you?

ARJUNA: Sorry Lord!

KRISHNA: I told you that all actions must be Spiritual because it is only Spiritual actions that would enable you to fulfil the purpose of life.

ARJUNA: Purpose of life? What is that?

KRISHNA: In one simple sentence it is this: From God you have come and to God you must return.

ARJUNA: I shall accept that Krishna, though I must confess that I do not really understand what You are saying! But even if that is the purpose of life, what has the *Atma* got to do with that?

KRISHNA: Everything!

**In this Chapter, Krishna has basically made two points, namely that life is a succession of actions, and secondly that all actions must be spiritualised. Why? Because that is the best way of achieving the purpose of life. All this is a prelude to connecting action with duty, and then aligning duty to the Nature of the *Atma.* Those linkages would slowly be unravelled as we go along.**

CHAPTER 3

# ACTIONS, GOD, AND THE *ATMA*

**The *Upanishads* wax eloquent about the *Atma* and *Brahman*, but until Krishna taught *Atma Vidya* [Knowledge of the Self] to Arjuna in simple language, this Supreme Knowledge was almost inaccessible to ordinary mortals. Picking Arjuna as a representative of an intelligent person but entrenched heavily in worldly affairs, Krishna takes him step by step through the amazing connection between ordinary life and God. As a part of that exercise, in this Chapter, Krishna would be speaking about life and its relationship to God/*Atma*.**

ARJUNA: Tell me Krishna, how is the purpose of life related to the *Atma*? Frankly, I cannot see any connection at all!

KRISHNA: That Arjuna, is because you are ignorant, I mean Spiritually ignorant. People imagine that life has been given to them for having a good time, for acquiring wealth, empire-building, enjoyment, sense gratification, etc. Wrong, wrong all the way!

ARJUNA: Krishna, I am simply amazed! Why then according to You, did God give life to humans?

KRISHNA: Ah, now you are asking a good question! You see

Arjuna, people do not realise that human birth is an immense blessing.

ARJUNA: In what way?

KRISHNA: You mean you do not know? I shall describe all that later; but for the moment, let me just say, human beings have incredible capability that no other living species has, and no species has ever enjoyed before in Creation. And why do you think God gave humans this capability? For something silly like mere pleasure seeking and hoarding wealth?

ARJUNA: Tell me please, why did God bless humans with a special form?

KRISHNA: I certainly shall.

You must have heard the *Vedas* declare: *Jantuunam, narajanmam durlabham*. Basically it means that human birth is rare and special; it is special because humans alone can comprehend there is a God who created this Universe. No other entity, inanimate or living species, has this ability. Further, humans alone have the ability to understand that they are a Spark of the Divine, and that life is given for refining and purifying human nature, cleansing it of all undesirable traits so that one could go back to God!

ARJUNA: Going back to God? What does that mean?

KRISHNA: Well, you know, don't you, that clouds are formed

from the waters of the ocean and that rain comes down from the clouds? What happens to this rain water? Some of it finds its way to a river and then via this river flows back to the ocean, thus completing the cycle. The rest of the water also does the same but takes a much longer route and therefore also a much longer time. In the same way, from God you have come, and to God you must return. That, in one short simple sentence, is the purpose of life. Of course different people will do it at different speeds!

ARJUNA: You make it all sound so simple! What do you mean by saying that to God we all must return? Where is this God and how does one get there?

KRISHNA: [Laughs] Ah, at last we are getting there! That exactly is what I am trying to tell you right now, and let Me do it slowly, one small step at a time.

Remember I told you that your true nature is the *Atma?* That automatically implies that the *Atma* within ought to be the guiding star of your life. Unless all actions become aligned to the *Atma*, life would be wasted.

ARJUNA: In what way?

KRISHNA: If actions are not in accordance with the Nature of the *Atma*, the purpose for which God gives man his life would be totally lost.

Arjuna, I can see you shaking your head!

Obviously, you are totally puzzled. It is not all that difficult to understand. Let us start by asking what is God, what is the *Atma*, and what is the difference between the two. People think they are different, but they are not; in fact they are both one and the same–just that two different names are used to describe the same Formless Supreme Entity, that is **BEYOND** Creation, and from which everything came later.

You see Arjuna, God has no form. He is Formless! And that exactly is what the *Atma* also is! So, God is *Atma* and *Atma* is God! As simple as that! Just two different names for referring to the same thing–what's so difficult about it?

ARJUNA: O Krishna, my head is really reeling! I mean, what about You? I thought You are God and You have a Form, a very beautiful one I might add. And now, You are telling me God is Formless!

Krishna, please have pity on me! Don't confuse me so much! I am already so confused about this war! Just tell me why I must fight!

KRISHNA: [Laughs] My dear Arjuna! I know your plight but don't worry; I am in fact trying to resolve all your doubts; just be patient and listen carefully. Your problem is that you are used to looking at actions from a purely worldly point of view; that would not do. You **HAVE** to bring in God, *Atma,* etc., because unless you intimately relate to the *Atma*, you would not be able to get back to God eventually, and remember, that is the sole purpose of life! By the way, believe it or not, for you, fighting in this war would be one huge step towards God!

ARJUNA: Really? Sounds too good to be true!

KRISHNA: Not when you understand all that I am trying to tell to you.

You scc Arjuna, you are highly confused at present, and it is to remove your Himalayan confusion that I am now imparting Supreme Knowledge, also called *Atma Vidya* or the Knowledge of the Supreme Self. If you grasp this, you would know everything that is to be known. Thereafter, you would have no doubts about anything, including how to act in any given circumstance. That is why this teaching of Mine is so very important!

ARJUNA: Krishna, forgive me please, but I am feeling utterly lost because You are telling me things I have never heard before!

KRISHNA: I appreciate your problem, Arjuna, but don't worry, soon you would be able to understand fully all that I am telling you.

ARJUNA: I am grateful to You for being so compassionate to me.

KRISHNA; Arjuna, you forget that Love and Compassion are My very Nature; in fact, they are your Nature too, and that exactly is what I am trying to tell you right now! Now let us get back to where we were.

Basically, God is Formless but when humanity is in deep trouble, God descends with a human form to help man.

To put it simply, from time to time, God descends as man so that man may rise to the level of God! Don't rush Me right now with a barrage of questions! I know you have many, and I shall deal with all of them later.

For the moment, just try to understand that though you have a body, you are **NOT** the body; rather, you are something Eternal and that Eternal Nature of yours is the **CORE** of your personality.

ARJUNA: Krishna, are You saying that there is something Eternal inside me, and that something is the *Atma*?

KRISHNA: Correct.

ARJUNA: And that this *Atma* inside is nothing but God? Which means that God is actually in me?

KRISHNA: Absolutely.

ARJUNA: Krishna, let us be serious. Are You saying that since the *Atma* is in me, I too am God like You?

KRISHNA: Indeed, and you have got the point!

ARJUNA: No Krishna, I have **NOT** got the point! How can I be God? I am Arjuna, right now a very confused Arjuna I might add.

KRISHNA: [Laughs] My dear friend, I **KNOW** you are confused, and that is why I am telling you all this!

ARJUNA: But Lord, what You are telling me merely adds to my confusion!

KRISHNA: Arjuna, I understand your problem; so, let Me do it all over again slowly, step by step. Will you promise to listen carefully?

ARJUNA: I sure do Lord, especially when You are so kind and compassionate to give me Your valuable time.

KRISHNA: Good, and now listen carefully. Point number one. In Creation, God created man as the end-point of the living species so that this one species can cognise, comprehend and understand the **SOURCE** of Creation.

ARJUNA: But Krishna, I know where the Universe came from; it came from You! I am aware that God created the Universe, and everything in it.

KRISHNA: Yes Arjuna, you may know that fact but you seem to forget it when it comes to brass tacks. Now if you **REALLY** knew that God created the Universe, then you should also know that God created you too.

ARJUNA: But I know that also!

KRISHNA: In that case, how come you do not know the purpose of life? If God created you, don't you think there was a purpose behind creating you?

ARJUNA: I agree that there was a purpose but why are You saying I don't know the purpose?

KRISHNA: I am saying that because you do not know how to act in the present circumstance!

Arjuna, know this to be true! The Universe is a stage and Life is a drama, a Cosmic Drama staged by God; and in this Drama, all are actors!

ARJUNA: Am I also an actor?

KRISHNA: Of course you are, and indeed everything in Creation is! Your problem is that you do not know that you are an actor and that in God's Drama, you are supposed to speak the proper dialogue instead of acting or speaking the way you wish!

ARJUNA: There you go again, confusing me totally!

KRISHNA: Arjuna! Stop interrupting me every second! Just listen to Me for a while, will you?

ARJUNA: Yes Lord!

**The conversation has now reached an interesting stage where the focus shifts from a single individual, namely Arjuna and what God expects of him, to the whole of humanity. It is**

**all done with a subtle touch of mystery and the suspense one expects from a great Director! No wonder for is not Krishna, the Divine Playwright, the Divine Director, and also the Divine Producer as well?**

CHAPTER 4

# DIVINE DRAMA EXPLAINED

**Krishna now explains that whether one likes it or not, the life of an individual is intimately tied to God's Master Plan regarding Creation. Arjuna is totally baffled and wants to know why God wants all these complications; Krishna patiently explains.**

ARJUNA: Krishna, forgive me but please understand my problem. When I expressed reservations about this war, You asked me to get up and fight. From there we have moved quite far away–to God's Drama, proper dialogue and all that. Is it any wonder I am totally lost?

KRISHNA: If you just listen to Me for a while, all would be clear.

ARJUNA: Very well, and now please tell me–this war that is just about to begin–is this also a part of Your Drama?

KRISHNA: Yes it is; otherwise, do you think this war would have even been thought of?

Arjuna, everything in Creation exists for a purpose that is a part of the overall Master Plan; and all beings are expected to play their respective roles in this Divine Play! Your problem is that you do not know that you are an actor and that in God's Drama, you are expected to stick to the correct dialogue instead of acting or speaking the way you wish!

ARJUNA: Krishna, please forgive me; kindly explain all this in a manner that this simple soldier can follow!

KRISHNA: [Laughs] I understand your problem! You see, when I created the Universe, I filled it with many entities; everyone of these came from Me and therefore, they are not only Divine in origin but also have the power of the Divine in them, to varying extents of course.

I am sure you have heard Vedic chants describing all this.

First came the five elements.

After the elements were created, physical matter emerged in various forms, like galaxies, stars and planets. And on the planets formed in due course, continents, mountains, deserts, rivers and oceans.

The stage was now set for life to emerge, first in a very primitive form. Life then slowly evolved to more and more complex forms. At the end of it all, after a long preparation, came the humans.

All this diversity originated from Me, and every bit of this vast diversity has the seed of Divinity latent in it.

That is why the scriptures say: From ONE came many.

You may say I separated Myself into diverse forms, some animate and some inanimate.

ARJUNA: Lord, why did You do that?

KRISHNA: That is a good question. I separated Myself from Myself so that I could love Myself!

ARJUNA: I don't follow that.

KRISHNA: Well, it is this way. Since every being has come from Me, every being is also filled with Love, at least in a latent form; and that is because I, the Ultimate Source, am nothing but Love.

ARJUNA: Yes, I have heard people say: GOD IS LOVE AND LOVE IS GOD.

KRISHNA: That is right. However, without a platform, Love remains somewhat abstract. For Love to manifest and have its play, a stage is required and that stage is the Universe.

ARJUNA: I see; so is that why You created the Universe?

KRISHNA: Exactly. Arjuna, you must have seen the mother bird feeding the young ones. That is Me in the form of the mother bird, loving Me in the form of little birds, through the act of selfless feeding.

Indeed, there is Love across species. Have you not seen a dog love its master?

ARJUNA: All that I can understand, but Lord, how does a tree love a man?

KRISHNA: Well, the tree serves man in so many ways; it gives shade, it gives fruit, and finally it gives up itself as wood; that too is an expression of My Love.

Seen this way, there is an expression of hidden Love almost everywhere in this Universe.

ARJUNA: Krishna, why all this? Why do You have to love Yourself in this complicated way?

KRISHNA: Arjuna, there are some things you should not question in such a dry and soulless fashion.

Children play all by themselves, making up things and talking to themselves, pretending to be many things at the same time, etc. All that play is a reflection of Divine Play itself. I play in the same way a child plays with itself. Why should I not?

ARJUNA: So Creation is a Divine Play or a *Leela*, and life a part of the *Leela* of the Lord?

KRISHNA: Absolutely!

ARJUNA: If life is all about You in some form loving Yourself in some other form, then how come there is so much hatred and violence? How come the Kauravas hate us so much and now want to fight with us?

KRISHNA: Ah, there we come to the great mystery of life!

ARJUNA: Krishna, You have lost me again!

KRISHNA: Well, it is this way. You see Arjuna, God is Perfect and Pure, but when He created the Universe, He projected Himself onto a substrate, made up by Space and Time. That is where some imbalance sets, which in turn leads to the kind of problems you just mentioned.

ARJUNA: So, the Universe is nothing but a projection of God, is it?

KRISHNA: Correct. Imagine a beautiful statue standing on a pedestal. A light is placed so that a shadow of the statue is cast on the ground below. The shadow is just a projection; sure, it would have many of the features of the original statue but many features would also be lost, while some others might appear distorted.

The Universe is like that. It is bound by Space and Time and therefore, certain aspects of Divinity do not find full expression; in turn, this leads to some imperfections, from which follow many complications.

ARJUNA: You mean all the created entities have some kind of behavioural traits due to the limitations of Space and Time?

KRISHNA: Yes, and these behavioural traits as you refer to them are called *gunas*.

ARJUNA: Let me see if I have got it right–You are saying that while the entities in Creation have *gunas* in them, You have none; am I right?

KRISHNA: Absolutely.

ARJUNA: Krishna, are *gunas* responsible for anger, hatred, etc.?

KRISHNA: Right again!

ARJUNA: But what about mountains, rocks, and so on? I can't see mountains getting angry!

KRISHNA: Ah, you see *gunas* operate at two levels, at the level of the gross and at the level of the Mind.

It is at the level of the Mind that problems like anger, greed, etc. arise and create immense trouble. That is why *gunas* are readily seen in animate beings like a tiger, for example.

ARJUNA: Krishna, let me get it straight; are you saying that it is the Mind that creates all kinds of problems?

KRISHNA: Of course! You are a hundred percent on the mark.

Arjuna, the Mind is a very powerful instrument that God has given to every single human being; however, it needs strict control. Without control, the Mind can be a deadly enemy; but with control, it can be a great friend.

ARJUNA: But why all these complications?

KRISHNA: Why not? These complications as you call them certainly make the *Leela* fascinating! It is to help man to sort out the problems he creates for himself via his Mind that I am here. If I were not here, would you be getting all this advice? Don't get lost by questioning God's "motivation". He knows very well what exactly He is doing and why. What you and all humans like you ought to do is to concentrate on following God's commands!

ARJUNA: I never knew all this!

KRISHNA: Well, at least now you are getting to know it all!

ARJUNA: That is true and I am really grateful to You for all that You are so patiently telling me.

**Although Krishna is describing the Universe as a stage for enacting His Divine Drama, later He would [implicitly] liken it to a huge Examination Hall, and all humans as candidates taking a Divine Test! Either way, it is all a part of how God allows His children to evolve spiritually, and become One with Him.**

CHAPTER 5

# THE IMPORTANCE OF FUNDAMENTAL DISCRIMINATION

**There is a basic difference between plays scripted by humans and God's Divine Drama. While in the former everything is pre-determined by the author, in God's play, there is flexibility at the micro level. This arises because God allows humans to decide how they would act. That decision is made by the Mind, and thus it is that the Mind plays a key role in determining one's Destiny. Krishna explains that the advice of the Mind should never be accepted without scrutiny and this calls for Spiritual or Fundamental Discrimination.**

KRISHNA: Arjuna, there is something more you should know about the human Mind. As I told you earlier, it is a gift of God and **unimaginably** powerful. What people normally call the Mind refers to the inquisitive, ambitious and creative part. It is this aspect that drives man to adventure, to start business and make money, to seek power, and to dominate. In addition, the Mind helps man to innovate and invent, making life easier and more comfortable.

Besides the curiosity and the ambition aspects, the Mind has a creative part too, that helps man to create music, paint, sculpt, produce literature, great works of art, and so on.

All this capability of the Mind is described as *medha shakti*, and this power or capacity is focussed mainly on the **EXTERNAL** world.

ARJUNA: Any problem with that?

KRISHNA: Yes there is.

You see Arjuna, Creation or *Prakriti* is full of diversity; and this diversity comes due to the *gunas*, to which I made a brief reference earlier.

ARJUNA: But what has that got to do with *medha shakti?*

KRISHNA: Everything.

ARJUNA: In what way?

KRISHNA: Let us start with the fact that since you, Arjuna, are also a part of *Prakriti* or Creation, you too have *gunas*. Thus, the way your Mind forms impressions about what happens in the world is very much influenced by your *gunas*.

ARJUNA: Is that why selfish persons often tend to be suspicious, mean, etc.?

KRISHNA: Correct. And I suppose you are aware that some people are very jealous! That too is due to *gunas*.

ARJUNA: Don't I know about jealousy! There is Duryodhana, the prime example!

KRISHNA: Yes, that is a good example of a person being under the influence of *gunas*.

Right now I have no time to tell you more about *gunas*, but you just take it from Me that the essence of it all is that worldly knowledge or *medha shakti,* while very important, is not enough.

ARJUNA: Why?

KRISHNA: Because *medha shakti* is influenced by the *gunas*, and there is the danger that a person can misuse the worldly knowledge that he has.

ARJUNA: If *medha shakti* alone is not enough then what more is needed?

KRISHNA: *Medha shakti* or worldly wisdom must be balanced by a moderating agency called the *Buddhi*.

ARJUNA: *Buddhi?* I have heard that term before but what exactly does it mean?

KRISHNA: *Buddhi* means Discrimination, not just worldly discrimination, but Fundamental or Spiritual Discrimination.

ARJUNA: Krishna, why is *Buddhi* important?

KRISHNA: Arjuna, let us examine your present problem. Right now, the stage is set for war, which did not happen all of a sudden. You know the full history. We tried to avoid this war by offering peace and compromise but that offer was rejected.

Now why did the Kauravas reject the peace offer?

ARJUNA: The Kauravas rejected our offer because they are greedy and want to grab every inch of land they can get hold of.

KRISHNA: That greed, Arjuna, reflects the absence of Fundamental Discrimination in the Kauravas. They simply do not know how to analyse a situation properly and arrive at the correct decision.

ARJUNA: I agree with that, but You cannot say that my refusal to fight is also due to lack of Fundamental Discrimination. In fact, I am using my discrimination to say that war will not gain us anything, especially happiness.

KRISHNA: On the contrary, Arjuna, you too are suffering from the same disease, and all I am trying to do is to cure you of that disease!

In a worldly sense, your standpoint and that of Duryodhana are certainly different. But when it comes to lack of Spiritual Discrimination, both of you lack it!

ARJUNA: Krishna, I am shocked and also pained that you equate me to Duryodhana!

KRISHNA: No Arjuna, it is not like that! You see, Spiritual Discrimination is required if one wants to perform right action and duty in conformity with *Sathya* and *Dharma*.

ARJUNA: Are You saying my refusal to fight is not in accordance with *Dharma*?

KRISHNA: That is exactly right!

ARJUNA: Oh my God! It looks like I am doing nothing right!

KRISHNA: Arjuna, listen to Me. I am not trying to find fault with you but merely helping you to correct yourself.

It is this way: Performing duty involves action; fighting is an action, and right now, it is your **duty** to fight!

ARJUNA: Can fighting be called a duty?

KRISHNA: If you are fighting for your kingdom, I would not quite call it duty. I am **NOT** asking you to fight for your kingdom; I am asking you to fight for *Dharma*!

Man must always uphold *Dharma*, and if he has to give up his life for doing so, then he must be prepared to do it. That is man's duty! Remember, this war is really between the forces of *Dharma* and *adharma*; it is clear, is it not, on what side you should be fighting?

ARJUNA: Krishna, those are strong words!

KRISHNA: Yes they are, and you must understand why I have said so.

ARJUNA: Krishna, it would appear that right-action, duty and *Dharma* are all strongly interconnected.

KRISHNA: Absolutely, no question about that. Arjuna, I understand your problem; you have been suddenly exposed to a whole string of words unfamiliar to you. It is therefore not surprising that you are not clear about the linkages between them. But don't worry, I shall make it all clear as we go along.

**As Krishna delves deeper into *Atma Vidya*, Arjuna begins to have more and more questions. The Compassionate Lord patiently answers them all, as we shall find Him doing in the next Chapter and the others that follow.**

CHAPTER 6

# THE ROLE OF *BUDDHI* IN MAKING THE RIGHT DECISIONS

**Continuing His explanation of the role played by the Mind, Krishna points out how the Mind could be a friend as well as a foe; this is where the *Buddhi* enters the picture. With the help of *Buddhi*, the Mind would be a friend and play a kcy rolc in making actions conform to *Sathya* and *Dharma*. But without *Buddhi*, Mind would quickly lead one to the slippery slope of disaster.**

KRISHNA: Arjuna, humans create problems for themselves by relying excessively on worldly intelligence or *medha shakti*. You are a very clever man; however, your smartness is mostly related to the external world.

ARJUNA: Wait a minute! We all live in the external world; should we ignore it and not pay attention to it at all?

KRISHNA: Did I say that? What I am saying is that while you must certainly pay attention to the external world, you must pay **MORE** attention to the *Atma*.

ARJUNA: Why?

KRISHNA: Because the *Atma* is Eternal while the world is only transient; besides, your true Nature is the *Atma*.

ARJUNA: On the other hand, Krishna, while my body may perish, the world goes on; it has gone on for thousands of years. How can one dismiss it so summarily?

KRISHNA: I am not asking you to dismiss the world totally. Everyone lives in the world; saints and sages have done so; and I too have incarnated in this very world. Therefore, one must not and **CANNOT** ignore the world. At the same time, one must not ignore the *Atma* either, because remember, it is the **VERY CORE** of one's being and Eternal too!

ARJUNA: Do You mean to say I refused to fight because I ignored the *Atma*?

KRISHNA: Indeed, that's exactly what happened!

ARJUNA: I do not understand.

KRISHNA: Arjuna, you refused to fight because you thought you were the transient body, forgetting that you are in fact the *Atma*. Such forgetfulness makes you get excessively attached to your relatives, friends and *Gurus*. This is nothing but *dehabhimaanam* or body-consciousness. The *Atma* has **NOT** guided your decision and that is the real problem; and that problem has come about because you lack Spiritual Discrimination!

ARJUNA: Krishna, are You implying that I ignored the connection between the *Atma*, *Buddhi*, and *medha shakti*?

KRISHNA: Yes indeed. God has blessed you with *medha shakti* for survival in the world. Survival is very important, and that precisely is why God has given you *medha shakti*. But that does not mean you should rely solely on it, ignoring the *Atma* as if it did not exist or matter. In fact, in all critical matters, the decision **MUST** be based on larger considerations related to the *Atma*, and that is where *Buddhi* helps.

ARJUNA: How exactly does the *Buddhi* help?

KRISHNA: Well, *Buddhi* is a link to the *Atma*. If this link is blocked or is not in good shape, you cannot get guidance from the *Atma*. The Mind then gets a good chance to misguide you, and you would end up doing something that is **NOT** your duty, and against *Dharma* itself. In short, if *Buddhi* fails to function, you can be sure you would soon be on the slippery slope to disaster.

ARJUNA: I am a little lost here because You have suddenly brought in the Mind. Where does the Mind come in, and how is it related to all that You said earlier?

KRISHNA: Good question! You see, a human being is made up of three distinct entities–the gross body, the subtle Mind, and finally the *Atma*, which is the source of everything. Among these three, the *Atma* comes first, obviously, since it is the source. Next comes the Mind; it is "shaped" out of the *Atma*, and is expected to take orders from the *Atma*; once the Mind receives instructions from the *Atma* conveyed via the pipeline *Buddhi*, the Mind then directs the senses and the body about how they should interact with the external world.

ARJUNA: I accept that but please tell me where and how I went wrong.

KRISHNA: When you said you would not fight, that statement was influenced by your Mind, which was guided by body-consciousness or worldly attachments. Your Mind never consulted or took any orders from the *Atma*. That was the fatal flaw.

ARJUNA: Alright, but please can you tell me once more where the *Buddhi* figures in all this?

KRISHNA: That's simple; as I just told you, the *Buddhi* is nothing but a pipeline between the *Atma* and the Mind. When the Mind is dominated by attachment to things of the external world, *Buddhi* becomes blunted; that is to say, the pipeline gets clogged.

ARJUNA: Oh I see. So, while *medha shakti* might give all kinds of ideas for action, one must always use one's *Buddhi,* or the capacity for Spiritual Discrimination, to check out if that action is right or wrong, is that it?

KRISHNA: Correct! *Buddhi* helps you to connect to the *Atma*, and that is why it is so very important.

You must connect to the *Atma* so that the *Atma* rules your life and not the Mind. That precisely is why the very first thing I told you was that you are **NOT** the body but the personification of the Eternal *Atma*.

This fact must never be lost sight of; only then can your actions be right.

ARJUNA: Krishna, can You summarise all that You have said thus far? Please tell me in simple words: What exactly is meant by right action?

KRISHNA: That's easy. Right action is that which reflects the Nature of the *Atma*. What is the Nature of the *Atma*? It is nothing but *Prema* or Pure Love.

ARJUNA: Krishna, You mean the Nature of the *Atma* can be described in just one word, Pure Love? Are you saying that if a person performs actions based on *Prema* or Pure Love then that person reflects the *Atma* within?

KRISHNA: Correct!

ARJUNA: And actions based on *Prema* would automatically be in complete harmony with *Sathya, Dharma, Shanti, Karuna, Daya, Ahimsa,* etc.?

KRISHNA: Absolutely!

ARJUNA: And the manifestation of all these virtues is absent when the pipeline called *Buddhi* gets choked?

KRISHNA: Correct once again!

ARJUNA: Krishna, why does *Buddhi* become blunted?

KRISHNA: Arjuna, tell Me, how is knife kept sharp?

ARJUNA: That is simple! We have to periodically sharpen the knife and make sure it never gets rusted.

KRISHNA: Right; in the same way, there is a discipline needed to keep the *Buddhi* sharp. If that discipline is not followed, then *Buddhi* can get blunted.

ARJUNA: Sorry, not clear!

KRISHNA: It is simple really. When man allows his Mind to be contaminated, *Buddhi* becomes blunted.

ARJUNA: How does the Mind get contaminated?

KRISHNA: Ah, that is a good question. You see Arjuna, by its very nature the Mind tends to wander in the external world, dragged there all the time by the senses.

ARJUNA: But Lord, it is YOU who have given us the Mind and the senses! Are not these faculties doing what they are supposed to do?

KRISHNA: Yes Arjuna, God did give humans the senses and the Mind, but does that automatically mean that man is using them the way they ought to be?

Let Me explain My point this way. God has given the tongue to animals and also to man, to help them with eating. But in the case of humans, the tongue also helps in speaking. Some people use the power of speech to abuse others. Did God ask them to do so? Do you think God gave them the tongue for that?

ARJUNA: I agree You have not given the tongue for saying bad things, but how exactly are we supposed to use it, apart from using it for eating?

KRISHNA: Simple! Use it for chanting the Name of God and singing His Glory! Is that so very difficult?

**The last point made by Krishna is incredibly important. For ordinary mortals, or, for that matter, even for very intelligent people who are unavoidably quite preoccupied with worldly affairs [like the Head of a State, for example], it is not possible to spend a lot of time pouring over the scriptures, absorbing all the intricacies. Krishna gives Arjuna the comforting news that it is really not necessary to do so, as long as one learns to constantly chant the Name of the Lord. Vivekananda said Meditation is merely the constant remembrance of the Lord, and *naamasmarana,* or constant repetition of the Name, is the easiest form of Meditation.**

**The question is often asked: The Lord is known by so many Names; which is the preferred one? Bhagavan Baba has answered it beautifully. He says [and this is captured in one of the Sai *bhajans*], "Chant any Name you like, but do**

so with Love and deep feeling in your Heart." Going through life without chanting the Name or *naamasmarana* is like driving a car without brakes! Gandhi attached great importance to *naamasmarana*, and that is why he was able to give up his body with the Name of the Lord on his lips, the importance of which Krishna would explain later.

Chapter 7

# ELEVATING WORK TO WORSHIP

**In this Chapter, Krishna exposes Arjuna to two important concepts. The first is that of Mind and sense control, and the second concerns elevating work to worship; the two are of course related. These days, Mind and sense control is often viewed by many as imposing unwanted restrictions and curbing one's right to do what one pleases. Such a viewpoint is totally misplaced and reflects a lack of proper discrimination. Imagine driving a car with no brakes, bad spark plugs, run-down batteries, a clutch that is not working, etc. Would anyone want to do that? Going through life without Mind and sense control is equally detrimental, where the purpose of life as stated by Krishna is concerned.**

ARJUNA: So Krishna, if I understand You correctly, just as he is misusing the tongue, man is also generally misusing his body, all the senses, and the Mind–is that what it all boils down to?

KRISHNA: That's exactly right.

Arjuna, the problem with you humans is that you do not appreciate why God has blessed you with so many wonderful capabilities.

Do you realise how dexterous the human body

is? Do you realise the amazing things the fingers can do? Do you really take time off to appreciate the power of the Mind with which God has blessed you?

I do not think so, for if man ever did that he would **never** waste his time indulging in useless actions all the time.

ARJUNA: Krishna, what then must man do?

KRISHNA: Frankly Arjuna, I am surprised that you are even asking such a question. Is not the answer to your question obvious?

Tell me, should man misuse every single organ of his precious body? How much better it would be if he used his time, senses and his most powerful asset, namely the Mind, to think good, see good, hear only good, speak only good, and perform only good actions?!

ARJUNA: If I read You correctly, You are asking for sense and Mind control, is that it?

KRISHNA: Exactly.

ARJUNA: Suppose I do all that You say; then what?

KRISHNA: What a question! If you did all that I said, you would be sanctifying your life, every second of it!

ARJUNA: And what good does that do to me?

KRISHNA: My dear Arjuna! Must you humans always do such cost-benefit calculations? You really do not know what's there in it for you?

ARJUNA: Krishna, I am sorry to annoy You, but please understand that till now no one ever talked to me about these matters. Is it any wonder that I am utterly ignorant?

KRISHNA: I understand Arjuna, and since you are My dear friend, I shall be more patient with you!

You see Arjuna, there is a deep reason for My insisting on right action and making sure it is tuned always to the *Atma*.

ARJUNA: And that reason is?

KRISHNA: The reason is good *karma* or good action would bring you closer and closer to God.

Arjuna, humans do not realise what for God has blessed them with life in human form. It is simple really; man has come from God and he must use his life to return to God–that is all!

ARJUNA: And performing good action, chanting the Name of the Lord always, etc., is part of this process of returning to God?

KRISHNA: Absolutely! Arjuna, have you heard the word *Yoga*? People interpret it in many ways but in truth, *Yoga* simply means union with God. It is thus a pathway to God. When *karma* is performed with good intentions, when it is utterly selfless, when it is driven by an intense love for God, then what you think is simple *karma* actually becomes *Karma Yoga!*

ARJUNA: Let me absorb this slowly. *Karma Yoga* simply means reaching God through right action?

KRISHNA: Right and **absolutely selfless action**, I might add.

ARJUNA: And further, *Karma Yoga* means action in conformity with the Nature of the *Atma*?

KRISHNA: Right again.

ARJUNA: And action that is in tune with the Nature of the *Atma* is automatically in full accordance with *Satya, Dharma* and *Prema?*

KRISHNA: Absolutely.

ARJUNA: Thank God I got at least some answers right! But now, I must let these teachings sink in and get absorbed.

KRISHNA: That is correct Arjuna, and that is why our ancestors stressed all the three aspects of learning; they are: first listening, then recalling and reflecting, and finally internalising or digesting.

And Arjuna, there is one thing more I must tell you concerning duty. People go about thinking they have all kinds of rights. That is **ABSOLUTELY** wrong. You have only one right and that is the right to perform your duty.

ARJUNA: And according to You, that duty must be performed in accordance with the Nature of the *Atma*; right?

KRISHNA: Correct. By the way Arjuna, this is what is called *Atma Dharma*. If that seems confusing, just remember that **action performed with Pure Love and in a totally selfless manner** is nothing but *Atma Dharma*.

ARJUNA: And the only right man has during life is to perform this duty or *Atma Dharma,* and none other?

KRISHNA: Absolutely.

ARJUNA: But Krishna, this is not fair!

KRISHNA: Why do you think so?

ARJUNA: Well, let us say there is a servant who works for a master. This servant is given duties that he performs diligently and honestly. Does not the servant have a right to expect fair wages?

KRISHNA: From a worldly point of view, maybe.

ARJUNA: But what other point of view comes in here?

KRISHNA: Ah Arjuna, you are forgetting the purpose of life.

ARJUNA: Krishna, be reasonable; we are talking of two different things. While You are talking about the purpose of life, I am talking about a servant who expects wages for work done properly and honestly. What's wrong with that?

KRISHNA: I did not say it is wrong.

ARJUNA: But You said that the only right a man has is the right to do his duty. I see some kind of a contradiction here.

KRISHNA: Yes Arjuna, you certainly would if you focus only on the world. It is to avoid that I am saying you should enlarge your vision to include the Creator.

ARJUNA: Why bring in the Creator? I am talking about a simple thing really, about work done and the expectation of fair wages for that.

KRISHNA: To you Arjuna, it might seem like a simple issue but it is precisely because of such simplifications that many problems arise. I have gone through some of it earlier but it looks like I have to repeat that again, perhaps in a different manner!

**The key sentence in this Chapter is Krishna's description of how to transform ordinary *karma* into *Karma Yoga*. We hardly realise how important, how practical, and how relevant this is in day-to-day life. By way of illustrating this, we reproduce below extracts from a letter written by a father to the Headmaster of the School where his son was studying:**

*He will have to learn, I know, that all men are not just and are not true. But teach him if you can, the wonder of books. But also give him quiet time to ponder the eternal mystery of birds in the sky, bees in the sun and flowers on a green hillside.*

*In school, teach him it is far more honorable to fail than to cheat...*

*Teach him to have faith in his own ideas, even if everyone tells him he is wrong.*

*Teach him to be gentle with gentle people and tough with the tough.*

*Try to give my son the strength not to follow the crowd when everyone is getting on the bandwagon... Teach him to listen to all men; but teach him also to filter all he hears on a screen of truth, and take only the good that comes through.*

*Teach him, if you can, how to laugh when he is sad. Teach him there is no shame in tears.*

*Teach him to scoff at cynics and to be beware of too much sweetness.... Teach him to sell his brawn and brain to highest bidders, but never to put a price on his heart and soul.*

*Teach him to close his ears to a howling mob... and stand and fight if he thinks he is right.*

*Treat him gently, but do not cuddle him, because only the test of fire makes fine steel. Let him have the courage to be impatient... Let him have the patience to be brave.*

*Teach him always to have sublime faith in himself, because then he will have faith in humankind.*

*This is a big order, but see what you can do. He is such a fine little fellow, my son!*

**You would be amazed to learn that this letter was written by Abraham Lincoln. Basically, Lincoln was telling the teacher about how he [the teacher] must do his duty; and when duty is performed in a selfless spirit with an eye on doing good to Society, it automatically becomes worship!**

Chapter 8

# PERFORMING DUTY IN THE SPIRIT OF THE *ATMA*

**A key point that Krishna implicitly introduces in the last Chapter is the importance of sacrifice, which is a key element of *Karma Yoga.* Despite what Krishna says, not many in this Kali Age would be prepared to buy that idea. We are so used to getting reimbursed, that we would strongly rebel at the notion of sacrifice. Yet, we scarcely realise how strongly, though in a subtle manner, the thread of sacrifice runs right across the Universe. In times of war, every country expects its soldiers to fight and even die if necessary. Even so, when it comes to a pinch, how many citizens are willing to do that? We are not advocating violence, but merely reminding that someone somewhere always slogs, so that others elsewhere may have a better life. In India, for example, a large part of the farming is still done using bulls for ploughing, accompanied by heavy manual labour. However, the wages that these farmers get is hardly ever commensurate with the amount of physical effort they put in. It is easy to discuss all this in terms of market etc., but all that veneer does not cover up the fact that many have to sacrifice so that few have it much better than the average. Can this be avoided? Yes, when everyone identifies with the *Atma.* Does that mean that sacrifice can be totally eliminated**

**or abolished? No, instead, every one sacrifices. But is that not like punishing everyone without exception? Not really, because when one identifies with the *Atma*, the one who sacrifices does not see it as sacrifice but as an act of Supreme Love. It is this important lesson that Krishna teaches in the present Chapter.**

KRISHNA: Arjuna, let us go back to the issue of fair wages that you brought up. In all that discussion, I never heard you mention God even once. Has God no place in the life of a human being?

ARJUNA: Krishna, please be reasonable! We are talking of two different things–You are talking about God whereas I am considering the case of an honest servant expecting fair wages. What is wrong with demanding wages? How does asking for fair wages imply that one is keeping God out of one's life?

KRISHNA: I did not say asking for what you call fair wages was wrong.

ARJUNA: But then You said that the only right a person has is to do his or her duty. And now, You are saying that while a person has a right to perform duty, the person has at the same time no right to expect fair wages for honest work done most sincerely! I see some kind of a contradiction here.

KRISHNA: You would certainly see a contradiction if you focus only on the world. It is to avoid that I am saying you should enlarge your vision to include also God.

ARJUNA: Krishna, once again I ask You: Why bring in God and create unnecessary complications? I am talking about a simple matter, of honest work and the worker expecting to be paid good wages for that.

KRISHNA: To you, Arjuna, all this might seem like a simple issue, but it is precisely because God is left completely out of consideration most of the time that many problems arise!

ARJUNA: O Krishna! You have lost me again! Looks like today, I am not able to understand even simple things! And if I may say so, You also are not able to follow the questions of a simple man!

KRISHNA: No Arjuna, it is **NOT** like that; I fully understand your question and I also know that millions like you have the same question. I shall therefore clear up this doubt once and for all, not only for your benefit but that of mankind as a whole. Now listen carefully!

ARJUNA: Thank You Lord, and I promise I shall pay careful attention!

KRISHNA: Good! Remember I told you that all actions, which means duty included, must be performed keeping the *Atma* in view?

ARJUNA: Yes, I recall You said something about *Atma Dharma* and things like that.

KRISHNA: [in a stern voice] Arjuna, do not talk of *Atma Dharma* so causally or lightly! It should be the very breath of your life, understand?

ARJUNA: Sorry Lord!

KRISHNA: That's better and now, pay careful attention.

You talked of a servant performing his duty; I am now telling you that duty must be performed in the **full** spirit of *Atma Dharma.*

ARJUNA: But Krishna, the servant in my example does exactly that! He is scrupulously honest, utterly loyal, works with great enthusiasm and utmost sincerity, and wants nothing but to please his master. Is that not the same as being true to *Sathya* and *Dharma?* What more would one want?

KRISHNA: Your model servant would no doubt get full marks where work performance is concerned; however, when he starts expecting payment, then he loses some marks!

ARJUNA: That is precisely what I call unfair. I simply fail to understand why the poor man cannot ask his master to pay good wages for the wonderful work he has done.

KRISHNA: Arjuna, I fully understand your difficulty; now

if you would give Me a few minutes without interruption, I shall clear your doubt fully!

ARJUNA: Once again Lord, Sorry!

KRISHNA: That's better. When I talked about *Atma Dharma*, it means that **all work and duty** must also be done with full *Atma Bhavam!*

ARJUNA: *Atma Bhavam?* What's that?

KRISHNA: *Atma Bhavam* is not a strange or a difficult word. Remember I said that *Atma* is God, and that God is Pure Love? If you put all these together, it adds up to the following: *Atma Bhavam* means working in the spirit of Pure Love, seeing God everywhere!

ARJUNA: Alright, let us suppose the man in my example is chanting the sacred hymn *Gayatri* all the time he is working; then what?

KRISHNA: That is very good, and it comes close to *Atma Bhavam;* however, it is not fully there!

ARJUNA: You are laying very tough conditions!

KRISHNA: Not really; can oil ever mix with water? Water alone will mix with water. Man has been blessed with life in human form so that he can return to God.

ARJUNA: Oil, water, mixing, returning to God? What is all this? Krishna please, I am simply lost!

KRISHNA: Arjuna, man having come from God is substantially Divine, about eighty percent one might say. However, during life, this percentage comes down because of contamination.

ARJUNA: And where does that contamination come from?

KRISHNA: You mean to say you do not know? It is all due to the Mind going astray, misled by the senses!

ARJUNA: Oh that!

KRISHNA: Yes, the Mind always tends to lead man astray. It happens life after life. However, it would not happen if man remembers the **REAL** purpose of life.

I wish to tell you once again that life in human form is given by God so that all contaminations of the Mind are totally eliminated. It is only when the Mind is purified that man can finally merge with God. Thus, humans should all the time seek to enhance mental purity. In fact, everything they do, every action of theirs, must, in someway or the other, enhance the purity of the Mind. That is what I meant by saying water alone can mix with water–understand?

ARJUNA: But Krishna, the man in my example is chanting *Gayathri* all the time he is working; what more can one ask for than that? Is he not sanctifying his time wonderfully? Does not chanting the *Gayathri* enhance purity of the Mind?

KRISHNA: Absolutely, but there is still one little thing missing and that is what makes all the difference!

ARJUNA: Something still missing? I do not understand.

KRISHNA: Don't worry; I shall explain it to you.

**Slowly, Krishna is leading Arjuna to the all-important concept of *Karma Phala Tyagam*, making work itself an end objective rather than the benefits that work might confer. That concept is unravelled in the next Chapter.**

Chapter 9

# DOING WORK FOR ITS OWN SAKE

**This is an important Chapter in which the key concept of *Karma Phala Tyagam* is unveiled and explained to Arjuna. Incidentally, without *Karma Phala Tyagam,* there is no *Karma Yoga.* So, if one wants to be a *Karma Yogi,* then one must be ready to practice *Karma Phala Tyagam!* That is the main message of this Chapter.**

ARJUNA: Krishna, while explaining how to work with *Atma Bhavam* and all that, You kept on insisting that there was something basic I was missing. What exactly is the point that is still eluding me?

KRISHNA: I am coming to that. Now most people are good by nature, and they certainly perform their duties with much earnestness, like the worker you cited. Some even raise work to the level of worship by chanting the Name of the Lord all the time. All this is very good and most commendable, but...

ARJUNA: It is that mysterious "but" that I am anxious to hear all about!

KRISHNA: Arjuna, you are so impatient that you do not even give Me a fair chance to explain! Anyway, let us forget that, for I fully understand how keen you are to acquire Higher Learning; for that, I strongly commend you.

Now where was I? Oh yes, I was telling you that while humans have a right to perform their duty, they have no right to expect any rewards. That bothered you and since then, we have not made much progress, spending most of our time in argument.

To get on with what I was saying earlier, suppose the servant in your hypothetical example keeps on working **WITHOUT** bothering about any wages?

ARJUNA: Are You really serious? How can that ever happen?

KRISHNA: Arjuna, forget about whether it can happen or not; just answer My question: Suppose the worker does what I say; what then?

ARJUNA: But Krishna, the man is working **precisely** for earning wages, so that he can feed his family and take care of it in the proper manner. How can he **not** bother about his wages? Does not the man have a duty to his family? Is he not supposed to provide for them?

KRISHNA: I never denied that, did I?

ARJUNA: Krishna, once again I am totally lost and this is beginning to be like a charade!

KRISHNA: Arjuna, all that you have said so far illustrates beautifully how people think and react when they are focussed only on the world, what it has to offer, etc. No, do not interrupt, and let Me finish.

It all comes back to **action and the motivation for action.** Actions mandated by one's duty in life are inescapable; they **have** to be performed, **AND** without any consideration of any reward.

Say there is sick old lady; is it not the duty of her son to look after her? Should the son abandon the old lady or, if he looks after her, demand reward, payment, compensation, etc.?

ARJUNA: Krishna, that is different! We are here talking about the duty that a son owes to his mother; how can one bring in payment, wages, rewards, etc. here?

KRISHNA: I am glad you understand that. A son owes a duty to his bodily mother and that duty **has** to be performed, **without** any expectation whatsoever of reward. You accept that? Fine.

Now let Me ask you: God has given you life and a human form; do you not owe anything to God?

ARJUNA: Did I ever say that man does not owe anything to God?

KRISHNA: Very well then. Let me make the good man in your example even better, by which I mean, this man is so noble and believes so strongly in seeing God everywhere, that he does his job seeing God in his master and offering his entire work to the God whom he sees in his master! That kind of an attitude might come as a shock to you and might even be dismissed by you as sheer lunacy; but before you do all that, just consider for a moment this possibility; suppose the man does exactly as I say; then what?

ARJUNA: Krishna, I must confess that this question is out of my world of experience. I am unable to imagine that there would be such a person, and even if there is one by chance, I simply cannot guess what would happen; except perhaps the master would say: "I am lucky to get this fool as my servant and maybe I can get work out of him without paying anything at all. How kind God is to me!" That, Krishna, is all I am able to think of.

KRISHNA: I knew you would give that answer, but do you know why you are saying so?

ARJUNA: Why am I saying so? Because that exactly is what happens in this world, which is full of selfish people!

Krishna, just recall; when You went to the Court of the Kauravas, You asked them to settle not for the return of all our kingdom but just **five** villages–five villages, that is all. And what did they offer You? Not even five pinhead of land!

| | |
|---|---|
| | You know the world is so full of selfishness; what answer then do you expect me to give? |
| KRISHNA: | Arjuna, I see your point. However, just because most people are selfish, does it mean you too should be? Just because most people forget what they owe to God, should you also do the same? |
| ARJUNA: | Krishna, all this is so new to me, and I simply have no idea of how to think or what to say in reply to Your questions! |
| KRISHNA: | Now at last we are getting somewhere!<br><br>Arjuna, what I am about to tell you might appear strange and even impractical. However, those are worldly considerations and I am not here to discuss worldly matters. As I mentioned earlier, My concern is with *Atma Vidya* or Knowledge of the True Self. Remember, that True Self or the *Atma* is your **REAL** Nature! Keep that in mind and pay careful attention to what I am about to tell you. |
| ARJUNA: | Thank You my Lord! |
| KRISHNA: | Good, and here in brief is what the book on *Atma Vidya* says:<br><br>1. All actions, no matter by whom it is performed and no matter what the circumstances, must **ALWAYS** be in tune with the Nature of the *Atma*. |

2. This automatically implies that action must be good, unselfish, full of Love, etc. That is what is meant by *Atma Bhavam.*

3. Notice that all this means that bad actions simply have **NO** place in the Rule Book! *Adharma* is ruled out, period.

4. Further, whatever is the action or duty that is performed, it must be done thinking of God.

5. It must not only be done thinking constantly of God but also offered to God.

6. In turn, this implies that one must not ask for reward. Offering first to God and then asking for reward would amount to converting the offering into a business transaction! Loving God is **NOT** a business proposition!

The bottom line is simply what I have been trying to tell you all along, and that is: Work as you must, and do your duty as you indeed must, in the position or situation that Destiny has placed you in.

**BUT DO SO WITHOUT ANY EYE WHATSOEVER ON THE OUTCOME OR ANY EXPECTATION OF ANY KIND OF REWARD, AWARD, MONETARY BENEFIT, OR EVEN WORLDLY PRAISE AND APPRECIATION.**

To put it all differently and in simple words,

*karma* must be done in the spirit of *Karma Phala Tyagam*. *Karma* means action, *Phalam* means fruit, and *Tyagam* means sacrifice. Thus, *Karma Phala Tyagam* simply means sacrificing the fruit of action. What that boils down to is just what I described in terms of not being bothered about the rewards, recognition, etc.

ARJUNA: Krishna, Your Rule Book may say all this, but…

KRISHNA: Ah, it is now **your** turn to use the word "but"!

Hold on; I know what exactly you want to ask. You want to know how one can survive, if one lived solely by the Rule Book–that is your question, am I right?

ARJUNA: Yes, that exactly is what I wanted to ask.

KRISHNA: Well, if God has put you in this world so that you make every effort to come to Him, would He abandon you when you are making a serious try?

Arjuna, take it from Me: You take one step towards God, and He would take a hundred, moving towards you. So, survival is **NOT** a problem as you imagine, provided you have **FULL AND TOTAL FAITH.**

ARJUNA: What You say may be true, but it is equally true that all this is extremely difficult for the masses. Meanwhile I have one doubt.

KRISHNA: What is that ?

ARJUNA: Let us say that a person does his duty, *karma,* or whatever, in the spirit of *Karma Phala Tyagam* as you describe it. Let us go back to the example of the servant and the master I brought up earlier. Suppose the master pays wages to the servant at the end of the month; should the servant refuse saying, "No, I did it all for God?"

KRISHNA: [laughs] Arjuna, you humans have a wonderful knack for misunderstanding, sometimes even twisting right into wrong. I am not saying you are doing it now, but the point is your doubt is the result of a lack of proper understanding. I only said the servant should not be hankering after wages and yearning for it; I never said he should refuse salary if it is given. On the other hand, what he should do is to receive it as a sign of God's Grace and thank Him for it. As someone said, "One praises the Lord for all the 'good' that happens to us and, at the same time, thanks Him for all the 'bad' that occurs to us, for each unfavourable event is in a way a wake-up call!" Hope it is all clear and now, what is your next question?

ARJUNA: From what You have said, I gather that while we should not go hankering after reward or success, we must simply accept whatever comes our way, including rewards and success, as signs of Grace. Am I right?

KRISHNA: Yes you are.

ARJUNA: Good, now what happens when people do their duty but expect rewards? Is it a sin to have such expectations?

KRISHNA: Ah, that is a good question!

**The question that Arjuna asks towards the end is very important, and indeed one that would occur to all of us. Krishna gives the answer in the next Chapter, where He would make it abundantly clear that one should not imagine that asking for wages or expecting a reward for hard work done is a sin. However, there is a catch. What is that? The answer is revealed in what follows.**

Chapter 10

# SACRIFICE OF EXPECTATIONS OF WORLDLY GAIN QUICKENS LIBERATION

**In this Chapter Krishna brings out two points. Firstly, expecting rewards, recognition, etc., binds one to the world, causing repeated rebirth with all the problems of life in tow. Secondly, if *Atma Dharma* is to be one's goal–and it had better be [!] for that is the *Gita's* main message–then doing work or duty with expectations of worldly returns on effort "invested" would be counter productive.**

KRISHNA: Arjuna, I am well aware that very few follow the principle of *Karma Phala Tyagam* strictly and in its totality. Most people **do** have expectations of various kinds when they perform legitimate actions or even their duty, and it is not at all a sin to have such expectations. However, while they may not be committing a sin as such, there still is a problem.

ARJUNA: Problem, what problem?

KRISHNA: It is like this. If people want success, rewards, recognition, etc., in return for the effort they put in, they might get it; and if they pray to God for rewards, He may even grant it. However, the problem is that success, rewards, awards, etc., are all connected solely with the external world and have very little to do with the main goal of human life.

ARJUNA: Is that where the problem is?

KRISHNA: Precisely. You see Arjuna, this world that everyone so easily and quickly imagines to be the only real thing, is actually full of duality or opposites, like pleasure and pain, success and failure, joy and sorrow, victory and defeat, hate and affection, etc. These opposites are intimately tied together and **CANNOT** be separated; they are like two sides of a coin. Thus, one cannot have only success, only happiness, and so on. If there are some successes, there would be some failures as well for sure. If one is happy now, he may be plunged into grief later, and so on. Tell Me Arjuna, is it ever possible to have a coin with just one side?

ARJUNA: I realise that one cannot have a coin with just one side, but leaving that aside, where is the problem? I am still not able to see any.

KRISHNA: Well, it is this way. Arjuna, you are a very good archer and a famous one too. The world knows about your skill and sings your praise. All that no doubt makes you feel very happy and proud. It is perfectly normal, as everyone would say, and I guess you would too. Now, suppose there is a new star in the horizon tomorrow; people would now start hailing and praising this new hero, quickly forgetting you and the great feats you performed in the past. How would you feel then?

ARJUNA: I guess I would feel pretty miserable!

KRISHNA: That exactly is My point.

You see Arjuna, in this dual world, nothing is permanent. If you are successful one day, you may encounter failure the next. If you are happy today, something might happen to ruin your happiness tomorrow.

Success and failure, pleasure and pain, joy and sorrow, exhilaration and misery, all these come in alternation. Thus, pleasure is nothing but an interval between two pains.

ARJUNA: That is an incredible statement and I never knew that before!

KRISHNA: You agree with Me, don't you?

ARJUNA: I have no choice since what You say is nothing but the truth. But then Krishna, unfortunately alternation of opposites is inevitable in the world, is it not? And I guess all we can do is to just accept that fact and live with it.

KRISHNA: It is certainly true that one has to live with the duality that world offers, but I ask you: Is it not possible to look **BEYOND** the dual world, even while living in it?

ARJUNA: Are You suggesting that there **is** such an option? If there is one such, what would that other option be?

KRISHNA: Well, before I start explaining that, let Me first tell you what the problem is, when you abandon the sacred principle of *Karma Phala Tyagam.*

Arjuna, when man performs actions with an eye on the fruit, one might say he is taking the eye off the ball.

ARJUNA: Why do you say that?

KRISHNA: That is simple and I am surprised that you are even asking that question. Remember what I told you earlier about the goal or the purpose of life? Do you think if you are focussed heavily on worldly rewards, attachments and the like, you would remember God and the purpose of life?

ARJUNA: Forgive me please, but I think there is a bit of contradiction here. Here we all are living in this world, and also performing our actions, duties, etc., in this very same world. We **HAVE** to be focussed on what we are doing; otherwise, things can go wrong. Who would want that? In fact, that would be against one's duty and I am sure You would agree with that.

And yet, here You are, saying: ***"Work without any eye on the reward."***

I see reward as an essential part of the world we live and work in. That being the case, how can one keep reward out of one's Mind? Can not one seek worldly rewards and God at the same time?

KRISHNA: Arjuna, your arguments are well made. Yes,

actions are meant to be performed in this world and there is no question that while one is doing something [which, by the way, ought to be good and not evil!], one must be totally focussed on what one is doing; otherwise, one is not performing one's duty properly–that is for sure. However, that does **NOT** mean that ambition should drive one's actions–that is My real point; and that really is what *Karma Phala Tyagam* is all about, not making ambition the sole motivator! I told you earlier that man must do his duty and leave all the rest to God! Can't you understand that?

ARJUNA: No I cannot! Krishna, please be reasonable. How can one give up ambition? It is a great motivator in life. Without ambition, a person would have no spirit, no life! He cannot survive and would simply perish.

KRISHNA: Well, where the world is concerned, one might appear to perish when one lacks ambition. However, God is not bothered about what opinion the world has; He makes up His own Mind, you know!

You have to look **BEYOND** the world and the present life, in order to get a better perspective of this crucial concept of *Karma Phala Tyagam.*

ARJUNA: Why?

KRISHNA: Here is why. You see Arjuna, ambition is a type of desire, and desire is something that invariably binds one to the world. It is therefore quite detrimental, where the true purpose of life is concerned; I would even go so far as to say that it is a very dangerous poison, especially in excess.

ARJUNA: Desire binds a person to the world? Desire is a poison? What on earth do those statements mean?

KRISHNA: It is this way: In life, desires, ambitions, etc. are always there; some of them might get fulfilled while others may not. The person therefore takes birth again, so that he or she can have another go at realising some of the earlier unfulfilled desires.

ARJUNA: I concede that might happen but how is that related to the problem You were mentioning earlier?

KRISHNA: Arjuna, are you not forgetting why God has given you life in the human form? Is it for returning to God or for the fulfilment of desires? If you spend your life chasing ambition, you not only get delayed in your return journey to God, but also get stuck with the pair of opposites, part of which might be sweet but part of which is certainly not, being bitter!

ARJUNA: [slowly] I see. You are saying that rebirth is caused or triggered by desires; and in every birth, one has an alternation of pleasure and pain. It is thus an almost endless cycle–is that it?

KRISHNA: That's exactly right. I should add that rebirth is **also** connected with settlement of accounts related to earlier births.

ARJUNA: Settlement of accounts related to earlier births? What's that?

KRISHNA: Well, during his life a man might have been very cruel, hurting and beating people. When he is reborn, he might be placed in a situation where he is now getting beaten! He might suffer pain in many other ways also.

ARJUNA: Is this what people often call the debt of past *karma?*

KRISHNA: Exactly!

ARJUNA: So the debt of *karma* also is responsible for rebirth? And if we get rid of that debt, there would be no rebirth?

KRISHNA: One must get rid of not just the karmic debt but also desires, because desires invariably lead to karmic debts; only then is one rescued from rebirth. In other words, you must wipe out past debts and make sure you do not incur new ones.

ARJUNA: And all that You said earlier like following *Atma Dharma* etc., would help in getting rid of this karmic debt?

KRISHNA: Absolutely! Besides, it would also put you on the road that helps you to escape from being born again, and all the misery that rebirth brings!

ARJUNA: You know Krishna, it is very strange that I am getting all these lessons here on the battlefield, just minutes before I start fighting. I wish I had been told all this earlier. It is so difficult to absorb these lessons right now, even as the opposing army is staring at me and wondering what is going on.

**The question might be asked: "What is to be gained by escaping rebirth, considering the 'heavy price' of sacrifice that has to be paid? Is the game worth the candle?" It is the answer to that question that Krishna is slowly leading up to.**

Chapter 11

# REAL HAPPINESS AND ITS VARIOUS IMITATIONS

**Few of us realise that whatever we do is subconsciously driven by a quest for happiness; that is because Bliss is our True Nature. However, we are NOT aware that Bliss is our True Nature, because we do not know that we are not the body-mind combination [read ego] that we mistakenly believe we are; rather, our true Nature is the *Atma.* Nevertheless, though we are not conscious we are the *Atma,* the thirst for happiness is latent within, and when the thirst manifests, we go looking for happiness of the wrong variety and in the wrong place; that is how all our problems start. This is the theme that Krishna deals with in the present Chapter.**

KRISHNA: Arjuna, let Me do a quick check at this point. How are you finding this crash course on *Atma Vidya?* Comfortable, or just managing?

ARJUNA: Krishna, if You want my honest opinion, it is leaving me absolutely dizzy!

KRISHNA: I understand your difficulty. When you hear about such matters for the first time, and that too in such a compressed manner, it can be somewhat overwhelming. But don't worry; you will soon get used to it and after that, you will never forget.

Money may come and it may also go; reputation may come and it may be lost. But once acquired, Spiritual Knowledge stays forever!

It looks like you want to ask a question; go right ahead.

ARJUNA: Thank You, Lord. Before I ask the question, first let me do a check.

As I understand it, desires have two consequences: firstly, they deflect our attention from the real purpose of life, which is to do everything possible to go straight back to God. Secondly, desires often make us do wrong things or indulge in adharmic acts, creating thereby a karmic debt burden. As a result, one is reborn; am I correct?

KRISHNA: A hundred percent on the dot!

ARJUNA: These desires–why do they arise at all?

KRISHNA: Now that is a real good question. You see Arjuna, man's core is the *Atma,* and *Ananda* or Pure Bliss is the Nature of the *Atma.* Thus, subconsciously, humans hunger all the time for the *Atma* because that is the way they can have permanent happiness or *Ananda.* But unfortunately, they are **NOT** aware that they have this hunger, and they compound the problem further by looking for permanent happiness in the wrong place.

ARJUNA: What do You mean?

KRISHNA: Well, let us start with a new-born child. Little babies often smile, just like that. They are too young to know anything about this world and yet they break into huge and beautiful smiles. Why? What are they so happy about?

ARJUNA: I never thought of that! What's the answer?

KRISHNA: The answer is simple. New-born babies are still in communion, shall I say, with God from whom they have come. God is always in Bliss and when babies are in touch with God, they too are happy. However, as they start growing up, they very quickly lose touch with God, and that is how all problems start!

ARJUNA: That I am not able to understand.

KRISHNA: It is very simple. As they rapidly grow, babies start focussing more and more on the external world. They are curious about everything they see. They grab anything they feel they can eat. If someone offers a toy, they reach out eagerly, and once they get a toy they become very possessive. Have you not seen babies fight over toys?

ARJUNA: Indeed, I have.

KRISHNA: The toy is a symbol of an object of the world. The baby really wants happiness but mistakenly thinks it is in the object called toy; that is why it hankers after it. After a while, the baby wants more and more toys; and so on it goes. The habit of accumulation and possession is acquired and it intensifies when the baby becomes an adult.

ARJUNA: You mean the desire for acquisition builds up?

KRISHNA: Exactly; from toys, the attention now shifts to land, property, wealth and even abstract entities like power and so on.

ARJUNA: Krishna, wait a minute please; if I understand You correctly desire is, in the ultimate analysis, is really a misguided quest for permanent happiness–am I correct?

KRISHNA: Absolutely! You see Arjuna, almost from birth, humans seek *Ananda.* However, very quickly, humans lose their way and make two basic mistakes.

ARJUNA: And those mistakes are?

KRISHNA: Mistake one: They look for permanent happiness in the wrong place. Mistake two: They think happiness is largely connected with material things.

ARJUNA: Two questions; firstly, what do you mean by looking in the wrong place?

KRISHNA: Well, do you agree the world is not permanent?

ARJUNA: I agree.

KRISHNA: Good. If the world is impermanent, how then

can you find *Ananda* or permanent happiness in an impermanent world? Is that not utterly foolish?

ARJUNA: What You say is absolutely true and I was not aware of it till now!

KRISHNA: That is because you seldom think about such matters. Indeed that is the trouble with all humans–they are so good in being busy about utterly useless things!

ARJUNA: Well, my next question is: You said that it was a mistake to think that happiness is connected with objects. Why is it a mistake to make such an association?

KRISHNA: Arjuna, **happiness is a state of being;** it is **NOT** in worldly objects. People take to drinking in the belief that there is joy in alcohol. Well, truly if there is joy or happiness locked up in alcohol, people should continue to feel happy even when they become physically sick due to addiction. Do they remain happy or do they feel miserable? How come by chasing happiness through drinking, they reach a state when they desperately want to give up drinking but cannot?

It is all a case of mistaken identity! Pursuing money, property, and power, people want to create for themselves a state of permanent happiness in this impermanent world. That, obviously, is impossible!

ARJUNA: [slowly] I see. It appears that since happiness is a state of being, and since the world is impermanent, it is meaningless to try and put oneself into a state of permanent happiness via objects and entities that are themselves temporary–is that it?

KRISHNA: Exactly.

ARJUNA: If things are as You say, then what must one do to seek *Ananda* or permanent happiness?

KRISHNA: Come on Arjuna, by now you should be able to answer that question yourself! Give it a try!

ARJUNA: Oh my God! You are putting me in a spot! Well, let us see; You said God is Bliss. Does that mean that the way to Bliss is to become one with God?

KRISHNA: Bravo! That's just superb!

Arjuna, take it from Me: **HAPPINESS IS UNION WITH GOD!** That really is what all *Yogas* are about. I spoke to you earlier about *Karma Yoga;* that is one path to Bliss; there are others too, and maybe we shall talk about them later.

For now, understand just this. Even while you are in this world with all its problems, you always can, if you make the effort, raise yourself to a state of being where you remain unaffected by problems, even as rainwater flows off a duck's back without wetting it. In that unaffected state, you can achieve a sublime and supreme union with God and experience Bliss.

ARJUNA: I suppose a prerequisite to all that is to learn to become detached from objects and entities of the world, even though one lives in the world and is fully involved in all sorts of worldly activities.

KRISHNA: Correct.

**The Message is loud and clear: If we want Bliss or non-stop happiness, then we must get rid of our tendency to identify ourselves with EGO and realise that our True Nature is the *Atma.* This is an ancient truth and has been known for ages. Yet, hardly anyone seems to be guided by that priceless lesson and benefit by it. Why? That is the topic that would engage Krishna and Arjuna in the next Chapter.**

Chapter 12

# MIND VERSUS CONSCIENCE – HOW ONE MISLEADS WHILE THE OTHER WARNS

**We now come to the crucial question: "Why, if we have all the information for achieving Eternal Happiness, are we not making use of it?" As Krishna explains, the answer to that puzzle is the Mind. Misled by the senses, the Mind can derail our quest for Bliss, offering instead a wide choice of fakes. If that is so, how to avoid being conned? That is what Krishna now teaches.**

ARJUNA: Krishna, from what You have said thus far, it appears that we humans have a great genius for giving God a low priority or even totally forgetting Him. Why is that?

KRISHNA: That is a great question; it is all because of the Mind!

ARJUNA: The Mind?

KRISHNA: Yes, the Mind! That is why I said earlier that Mind and sense control are absolutely important.

ARJUNA: Oh I see. If Mind and sense control is so very important, then please tell me more.

KRISHNA: Of course I shall. Let me start with the fact that what is called Mind, is really a very complex entity, having evolved from something referred to as the brain.

ARJUNA: So the Mind is something more than just the brain, the physical organ within our body?

KRISHNA: Correct. Now the brain has some cognitive abilities, and it operates in conjunction with the senses. Together, the brain and the senses function as one integral system, in which the senses perform some part of the action while the brain performs the rest. All this is of course, as ordained by God.

Even lowly living species have some senses and a primitive form of brain. Do you know why God has given all this to all the species right up to humans?

ARJUNA: Is it for survival?

KRISHNA: Exactly. The senses gather information from the external world, and pass on that information to the brain; the brain then examines the information and interprets it.

ARJUNA: What happens after that?

KRISHNA: After receiving information from the outer world and analysing it, the brain then gives instructions to the senses and various organs of the body as appropriate; together, these instructions then form a response to the signals received earlier.

ARJUNA: Krishna, we have five senses but only one brain. Does that mean that the brain is common to all the senses?

KRISHNA: That is obvious, is it not? However, there is meaning in your question. In fact, keeping the implication of your question in view, our ancients said there were five organs of action and five organs of perception; the former were called *karmendriyas* while the latter were called *jnanendriyas*. Actually, the five organs of perception are all physically embedded in the brain; one might say that different parts of the brain are "attached" to the different senses.

ARJUNA: But how is all this connected to the Mind?

KRISHNA: Patience, and I am coming to that! Now, the brain of lower species is largely able to cognise only matters related to the **EXTERNAL** world, and this point is crucially important. Humans have a much **HIGHER** cognitive ability that goes **FAR BEYOND** the brain–that is where the Mind comes into the picture.

ARJUNA: Krishna, hold on for a minute please; when you say external world, what precisely do you mean?

KRISHNA: You asked me a question, and so let Me ask you one in return!

When I say your Mind, where is this Mind? Is it on top of the chariot we are in? Or is it in the sky? Where is this Mind?

ARJUNA: I guess, it is in me.

KRISHNA: Alright, but where exactly within you? Is it in your head, shoulder, heart, lungs–where exactly is this Mind?

ARJUNA: Frankly, I cannot answer that question.

KRISHNA: Well, here is another. We both use the word God. I suppose you generally understand what that word means. Now take a tiger. The tiger would surely understand about things on the earth, to some extent that is; but do you think the tiger can ever understand what God means?

ARJUNA: [laughs] That is a good one; a tiger being conscious of God!

KRISHNA: Arjuna, are you aware that unknown to you, you uttered an important word?

ARJUNA: Me? I did that?

KRISHNA: Yes, you used the word conscious. Arjuna, the word conscious means to be aware, and awareness is very important in Spirituality. In humans, there are actually three levels of awareness.

ARJUNA: Three levels of awareness? I never knew that! Now why should there be three levels? Would not one do?

KRISHNA: My dear Arjuna, don't you know that God never does anything without a purpose?

ARJUNA: Sorry Lord.

KRISHNA: Good, and now listen to Me carefully. The first level of awareness is described using the word conscious; being conscious essentially means being aware of the **EXTERNAL** world. Sometimes, when one is in a shock, one loses

| | |
|---|---|
| | consciousness; it means that the person is simply not aware of what is going on around him/her. |
| ARJUNA: | Yes, Krishna, I know that when a person suffers a very big injury, sometimes the person becomes unconscious. |
| KRISHNA: | That is right, and God makes that happen so that the person does not feel acute pain. |
| | The next level of awareness is related to knowing clearly the difference between right and wrong, *Dharma* and *adharma*. The agency which creates such an awareness is called **CONSCIENCE.** Humans alone are blessed with this kind of awareness. |
| ARJUNA: | If I get You correctly, apart from being conscious of the external world, an ability that all lower living species also possess, humans are special in that they have within them an agency called Conscience that makes them aware of what is good and what is bad. Since this Conscience cognizes aspects of thinking which go on **WITHIN** a person, it is quite distinct from the ability to be aware of what is external to the person–am I right? |
| KRISHNA: | Hundred percent! You know Arjuna, when a tiger kills a person, no one says it has committed a sin. |
| ARJUNA: | So I suppose a tiger does not have karmic debt like humans have. |
| KRISHNA: | You are exactly right. God has given humans a |

Conscience so that they can steer away from bad acts, and thus avoid unnecessary karmic burden. In fact, the Voice of Conscience is nothing but the Voice of God Himself, speaking from within.

ARJUNA: Is that why people say: "Listen to your Conscience?"

KRISHNA: Absolutely, and maybe you have also heard the saying: "It is only in the depths of silence that one can hear the Voice of God."

ARJUNA: No, I have not heard that; what does that statement mean?

KRISHNA: The word silence is used here not in the literal but in a metaphoric sense. What is meant is that mental noise must be brought down so that one can hear clearly what one's Conscience is saying.

ARJUNA: What do you mean by mental noise?

KRISHNA: You know, normally the human Mind is very restless; it wanders, and keeps thinking about all sorts of things. Such random chatter of the Mind makes it very difficult for a person to focus intently on one's Conscience and hear what it has to say.

ARJUNA: I suppose that is one of the reasons why You want strict sense and Mind control.

KRISHNA: That is correct. By the way, I hope you have noticed an important difference between being conscious and having a Conscience.

ARJUNA: What is that?

KRISHNA: The capacity for being conscious is all about the senses, whereas Conscience is something **BEYOND** the gross. Maybe we shall come to that later.

ARJUNA: Is what you call Conscience the same thing as God?

KRISHNA: Do you doubt it? Conscience is one of the many names given to God. Since Conscience is within, God is also called the Indweller.

ARJUNA: Does that mean that God is present in all humans as Conscience?

KRISHNA: Of course! Do you think God would be partial?

ARJUNA: Krishna, there is something I do not understand here. You say that God is within me; fine. You also say that God is within each and everyone of the tens of thousands we see assembled here on the battlefield. What I want to know is whether each person has his/her own God or is the same God present in all?

KRISHNA: [laughs] What a question?! Arjuna, how can there ever be many Gods? There is only one God and He is Omnipresent, that is all!

ARJUNA: [slowly] Oh I see.

KRISHNA: No Arjuna, you do not quite see and that precisely is why you raised the last question. When a person becomes fully aware that there is only one God, and further that this God is indeed in all, he attains the third and the ultimate level of awareness.

ARJUNA: Any particular name for this state of awareness?

KRISHNA: Yes there is, and it is called **UNIVERSAL** or **PURE CONSCIOUSNESS**.

ARJUNA: That was a real heavy dose and I need to absorb it slowly!

**The take-home lesson of this Chapter is: The "Ego-aspect" of our Awareness would try to get us pegged to the world, and in the process would blunt our Discrimination. The way out of this is to rely more on our Conscience, which is really God, the Indweller, constantly acting as our Spiritual Adviser. Krishna then goes on to point out that, we must not limit our perception of God by regarding Him merely as a personal friend and adviser, which of course He always is. God is much more, the Universal Consciousness or the all-pervading *Atma*. Later, Krishna would elaborate on the Omnipresent and Omnipotent God.**

Chapter 13

# ALL ABOUT THE LOWER AND THE HIGHER MINDS

**The word Mind that we use so very often is a very subtle concept with many nuances. In this Chapter, Krishna explains two basic aspects of the Mind called the Lower Mind and the Higher Mind respectively. To know what exactly they are and the roles played by them, let us join Krishna and Arjuna.**

ARJUNA: Krishna, slowly most of the things You are telling me are beginning to fall into place. However, it would be sometime before I am able to internalise them all.

KRISHNA: Don't worry Arjuna, take your time. Just make sure you do not let these teachings slip out of your mind–that is all!

ARJUNA: Thanks for the warning Krishna, and I shall try to be careful about that. Meanwhile, now that You have mentioned the word Mind, I want to know about the role of the Mind and of the Conscience, and the differences, if any, between the two.

KRISHNA: You have raised a good point. You see Arjuna, what is often loosely referred to as the Mind is a subtle entity quite distinct from the gross body. The Mind has two aspects to it really, and some scholars refer to these two aspects as the Lower Mind and the Higher Mind respectively. In a larger sense, both these "two Minds" are, in fact, aspects of the *Atma* but operationally it certainly is convenient to make this distinction.

ARJUNA: And what do these two aspects do?

KRISHNA: The Lower Mind is essentially what I earlier referred to as *medha shakti.* Remember *medha shakti,* which is the fountainhead of all worldly skills and creativity?

ARJUNA: Yes I do.

KRISHNA: As for the Higher Mind, it is nothing but the *Atma* in its full glory!

ARJUNA: [nodding his head and speaking slowly] And I suppose when the Conscience speaks, You would say it is actually the *Atma* speaking.

KRISHNA: Correct.

ARJUNA: Now let me get back to Duryodhana. Tell me in simple words why, if the *Atma,* Conscience, call it what You will, is present in him also, why is he so wicked?

KRISHNA: That is a good question because it illustrates what happens when a person gets stuck at the level of the Lower Mind, and further allows it to get corrupted.

ARJUNA: Corrupted by what and how?

KRISHNA: Corrupted by the deadly enemies of man, who else?

ARJUNA: And those enemies are?

KRISHNA: They are–and take note of this very carefully–*kama* or desire, *krodha* or anger, *lobha* or greed and miserliness, *moha* or attachment, *mada* or pride, and *matsarya* or jealousy. Enough for you? If not, here are two more: *ahamkara* or ego and *mamakara* or the sense of mine.

ARJUNA: Where do these "enemies" hang out, and how do they trap humans?

KRISHNA: That is a very important question. These deadly enemies hide in the "crevices, nooks and corners" of the Lower Mind, and they surface only when there is darkness, Spiritual darkness I mean. You have seen cockroaches, have you not? They seldom come out during daytime; but when it is night and dark, these creatures come out and wander freely.

These enemies of man act like touts, who relentlessly try to tempt the Mind into wrong ways, by dangling all sorts of attractions, and promising amazing excitement, unlimited happiness, etc. They will stop at nothing, in their effort to conquer and subjugate the Mind, and make it a total slave!

ARJUNA: Sounds frightening! But, what exactly do You

mean by Spiritual darkness?

KRISHNA: Arjuna, suppose a person falls into bad company; you know what happens, don't you? The person becomes immersed in seeing what is bad, hearing what is bad, talking what is bad and above all, thinking what is far from good. There is an overall corrosive effect, and that is what happens when one keeps company with those who have shut God out from their lives. Net result? The purpose of life is totally forgotten.

ARJUNA: So, if I understand You correctly, Spiritual darkness sets in when one forgets God–have I got it right?

KRISHNA: You have, and I might add that such darkness prevails when the enemies of man drag the Mind into alleys and by-lanes where all these "establishments" offering excitement, happiness, etc., operate.

ARJUNA: But why does man get tricked in this fashion? Whatever happens to the Voice of God, speaking from within? Why does not God warn the pilgrim not to go astray?

KRISHNA: Do you think God sits idly and watches all this? Not at all; He always sends His warnings; it is man, drunk with desires, who shuts out the warning. I thought I had already told you that when the Mind is busy wandering, the Voice of God gets smothered. Blame man and not God!

Listen Arjuna! For a moment, forget God, forget Conscience and all that. Just consider a father who is trying to advise his son who is keeping bad company. The father tries hard to give good advice, while the son stubbornly refuses to listen. You are familiar with that kind of scenario, are you not?

ARJUNA: Yes.

KRISHNA: The case of people not listening to the Voice of Conscience is something similar to that. Conscience says something, while the enemies of man hiding in the crevices of the Mind keep up a barrage of bad advice, making every evil suggestion they give sound so attractive and beneficial. And when the person is weak, he succumbs and listens to his enemies rather than to God, **who is the only true friend one has.**

ARJUNA: Krishna, does that mean Duryodhana is evil because he is **bent** on ignoring his Conscience?

KRISHNA: Yes, and you have put it succinctly.

Arjuna, it is not that God is present in some and absent in others. God is present in **ALL;** however, while some listen to the Indweller, others do not. Thus it is that you have good people and not so good people in this world.

ARJUNA: Basically what You are saying is that even though God, playing the role of Conscience, is constantly giving good advice, some people are hell bent on ignoring it; is that it?

KRISHNA: One hundred percent correct.

ARJUNA: Why at all does such a thing happen in the first place?

KRISHNA: Before I answer that, tell me: What are the three fundamental entities making up a human being?

ARJUNA: Let me see.... Is it the gross body, the subtle Mind and the *Atma?*

KRISHNA: Correct. Now tell me, what should be the hierarchy amongst these three, that is to say which should come first, which should come next and which should come last?

ARJUNA: I am not too sure but let me make a guess. Is it the *Atma* that should come first?

KRISHNA: Any doubt about that? Remember, *Atma* is God and God should always be your first priority! After the *Atma* comes the Mind, the body and the senses coming last.

ARJUNA: All right, we have this hierarchy, but what exactly does it mean in practice?

KRISHNA: You mean you cannot figure that out? Well, it is this way. Let us start with the senses gathering some information about the outside world and passing it on to the Mind. The senses tell the Mind, "This fellow is hurling abuses at you.

What action do you advise?" What would follow if the Mind decides to respond right away? Can you tell me?

ARJUNA: I guess the person being abused would immediately get angry.

KRISHNA: Indeed, but do you know why he would get angry?

ARJUNA: What do You mean why does the person get angry? What else do you expect this fellow to do when the other person is hurling abuses?

KRISHNA: I think you have missed my point. You see Arjuna, this person is responding to the abuses by getting angry because his Mind has been conditioned by enemy *krodha* to do just that. On the other hand, if the Mind had referred the matter to the *Atma* via the channel called *Buddhi*, the *Atma* would have said, "Just ignore what that person is saying. He will soon run of steam and simply go away!"

ARJUNA: If I get You right, basically what you are saying is that if the *Atma* is sidelined and the Mind begins to dominate the personality all on its own, then the Voice of Conscience is never heard.

KRISHNA: Exactly, and furthermore, when the Conscience is shut out, *kama, krodha,* etc., rush out from the crevices in which they are hiding to give company to the Mind! Duryodhana is keeping bad company, and that really is his big problem!

Do you understand?

ARJUNA: I think I am beginning to; let me check if I have got it right. Basically, the Mind should be subjugated to the *Atma.* If one fails to do that, then there is trouble for sure.

KRISHNA: That is exactly why I kept telling you earlier that Mind and sense control is very important for the Spiritual seeker; otherwise, man would get lost. Like everyone else, this fellow Duryodhana too wants happiness. However, misled by the bad company he is keeping, he is looking for happiness via power and position. In other words, he is getting conned and falling for fakes! One must really feel sorry for him!

ARJUNA: As I see it, the question now becomes: "How to turn the Mind towards the *Atma* or God?" Please tell me the answer to that.

KRISHNA: You have narrowed down the issue neatly.

The answer to your question is simple really. You see Arjuna, the Spiritual Heart is like a lock and the Mind is like a key. You know about locks and keys, don't you? If you turn the key one way, the lock opens; if you turn it the other way, lock snaps shut. It is the same with the Mind. If you let it go towards the world, you will end up with misery and suffering for sure, though things might appear different initially. On the other hand, if you turn the Mind towards God,

He would come towards you. The faster you go towards Him, the faster He would come, almost running towards you!

ARJUNA: Why would God do that?

KRISHNA: What a stupid question! Arjuna, man may forget God, but God would never forget man. Man may not love God, but God would always love man; that is His Nature!

**It should now be clear that the Lower Mind is really a reflection of our Ego-self or lower self, while the Higher Mind is likewise a representation of the *Atma* or the Higher Self [also simply called the SELF]. Most of us are trapped at the level of the lower self, thanks to the dominance of the Lower Mind. Life is all about going past that barrier, and that is where sacrifice, sense and Mind control, giving up attachments, etc., come into the picture. All this might appear impossible to achieve but it is in that context that Krishna has given us all a tip–to chant the Name of the Lord constantly. More assurances and guarantees follow in the next Chapter.**

Chapter 14

# GOD'S AMAZING ASSURANCE TO HUMANS

**The main message of this Chapter is an extraordinary assurance that Krishna gives in the *Gita* in the Ninth Chapter. It comes almost bang in the centre, and Bhagavan Baba has appropriately called it the fulcrum of the *Gita*. What is needed is for us to make that teaching the fulcrum of our lives!**

ARJUNA: Krishna, by Your Grace, I have learnt many things I did not know before. But there are a few things I am still not very clear about.

KRISHNA: What's your problem?

ARJUNA: Thanks to wonderful gift called the Mind or *medha shakti* if You prefer, man has amazing capabilities. And yet he seems to so easily fall a prey to his enemies; how come?

I mean this fellow Duryodhana; he is very clever, has studied under a *Guru* and has also been exposed to the scriptures. Yet he seems to be utterly blind to even basic values and the elementary requirements of decency. How come?

KRISHNA: You have raised a very good point.

| | |
|---|---|
| | Arjuna, there is something very important you must know. Without self-control, the Mind is **easily** dragged by the senses into the external world. Once dragged out there, it is a simple job for desires to enslave the victim. |
| ARJUNA: | What happens then? |
| KRISHNA: | Well, one thing leads to another and soon there is a free-fall. Desire often leads to jealousy, which in turn leads to anger. From anger arises delusion, which quickly gets the Mind completely confused. From then on, it is a slippery slope. In the end, there is a loss of reason and when reason is gone, it is only a short step to complete ruin. |
| ARJUNA: | You mean when anger grips a person he becomes blind to reason? |
| KRISHNA: | Does that come as a surprise to you? Anger can swiftly become hate, rapidly building up to **blinding** fury. At that stage, the person becomes insane, at least temporarily. Are you aware how much damage can be caused by temporary insanity? |
| ARJUNA: | Any way of quenching this fire or blaze? |
| KRISHNA: | Sure, there is a way. |
| ARJUNA: | And that is? |
| KRISHNA: | *Prema.* Remember *Prema?* |

ARJUNA: Yes I do, it is Selfless Love, is it not? And how does *Prema* manage to do the magic?

KRISHNA: *Prema* does wonders because it is Divine. Arjuna, don't you realise that there is no limit to the Power of God?

ARJUNA: Amazing! How come we humans are all ignorant about it?

KRISHNA: That, in fact, is the greatest tragedy! Man is the very embodiment of Divine Love, and yet he seems to be hardly aware of it. That is because you people are all busy in being totally absorbed in this transient world, ignoring what God is ever so ready to give you!

ARJUNA: I suppose that misled by the senses, the Mind makes us lose our way to God; and it would appear that as a result, we get caught up in the cycle of repeated births and deaths.

KRISHNA: That's exactly right.

ARJUNA: What happens to a person who, say, has wasted his or her life, as the case may be? The person dies; what next? I mean how exactly does the process of rebirth occur?

KRISHNA: Good question. Let us say that when this person dies he is cremated; the gross body is burnt, and, as they say, returned to the elements. Being subtle, the Mind cannot be so burnt. As for the *Atma,* it is subtler than the most subtle. It is beyond all forces in Nature; wind cannot blow it, fire cannot burn it, water cannot wet it, nor can a knife cut it!

ARJUNA: Does that mean that the Mind and the *Atma* survive death?

KRISHNA: Of course; not only that; after death, the *Atma* that was encased in the human body prior to death and the Mind, together form a complex called the Subtle Body. At the time of death, this Subtle Body cuts loose from the gross body and simply floats away; it moves on.

ARJUNA: Floats away and moves on? Where does it go and what does it do?

KRISHNA: Well, it goes around looking for a new body, that's what it does.

ARJUNA: Is that for the purpose of being born again?

KRISHNA: Correct.

ARJUNA: But Krishna, how does this Subtle Body choose a new body? Does it just move into the first foetus it comes across?

KRISHNA: Not at all. On the contrary, something very interesting happens.

ARJUNA: Which is?

KRISHNA: It is this way Arjuna. Let us say there is a man who is very cruel by nature and takes great pleasure in hurting people in all sorts of ways. When this man dies, his Subtle Body would choose a foetus in such a way that after birth, the person is now at the receiving end. This is what is meant by the settlement of karmic debt.

ARJUNA: Let us say a person is born blind as a result of his past *karma.* Now this blind child would be a great problem for the parents. Why should they have to pay a price even as this person is settling his karmic debt?

KRISHNA: Good question. Actually, when a Subtle Body enters a foetus, there is a beautiful overall karmic balance at play.

ARJUNA: What do You mean by that?

KRISHNA: I mean that every birth involves a delicate balance between the karmic debt of the child that is born **and** the karmic debt of the parents as well. That is the beauty of the Law of *Karma*–there is an amazing balancing process that goes on all the time.

ARJUNA: Krishna, this rebirth business; the way You describe it, it seems to be endless, which is rather frightening. Not everyone is pure evil; surely every person does some good at some time or the other. Don't people ever get any plus points for being good?

KRISHNA: You have brought up an interesting point Arjuna. What you call good action **does** earn merit or bonus points called *Punyam;* I am sure you have heard that word.

ARJUNA: Yes I have; so my question is: Does not the *Punyam* earned in earlier birth have any effect?

KRISHNA: Of course it has an effect. Basically, things happen this way. Thanks to the *Punyam* earned earlier, in the next birth, the person concerned is placed in a position wherein he or she has opportunities to improve the *Punyam* account, shall I say? Of course, whether or not the person makes use of this chance depends entirely on the way the Mind functions, and the way the person concerned responds to the advice from the Conscience. If the person improves his or her *Punyam* record, then there is progress.

In this way, life after life, through various ups and downs, there is a continuous process of refinement and a slow progress towards God.

ARJUNA: That is nice to hear; but on the other hand, the person could also slip, and it could be a case of one step forward and two steps backwards.

KRISHNA: That might well happen; it is up to people to make sure that does not happen.

ARJUNA: Let us say that life after life, a person struggles and keeps making progress. But even after that, I cannot see anyone becoming perfectly Pure. If that is the case, how can one ever merge with God who is Perfect and totally Pure?

KRISHNA: Ah, this precisely is where God's Grace enters the picture.

ARJUNA: What does that mean?

KRISHNA: Have I not told you earlier that if you take one step towards God, He would take a hundred steps coming towards you? Well, if a person makes a serious effort and has full faith in God, then you know what God would do?

ARJUNA: Please tell me; I am so eager to know!

KRISHNA: I certainly shall.

Arjuna, this is what God would do. He would bend, reach out and simply pull the person from bondage, liberating that person forever.

ARJUNA: That's wonderful!

KRISHNA: That is not all, for there is something more.

ARJUNA: What is that?

KRISHNA: Now listen to this very carefully, for by strictly adhering to what I am now about to say, anyone, no matter how far a person thinks he or she is from God, that person **CAN** come to Me for sure, within one lifetime!

ARJUNA: And what is that magic formula?

KRISHNA: It is a simple formula really and there is no magic about it.

All one has to do is this: ***Think of Me always, and chant My Name incessantly; I shall then step in and take care of the rest.***

ARJUNA: Say that again please?

KRISHNA: Here it is Arjuna.

***If a person constantly worships Me and thinks of Me all the time with no other thought, then I shall bear the entire burden of that person's welfare.***

Arjuna, do you understand what that means? Simply by thinking of Me all the time, you can get all the help you want to avoid being reborn. Can you get a better deal, to get out once and for all from this recurring cycle of birth and death?

You know something? God is always ready to help man; the problem is that man does not seek God's help, in fulfilling the purpose of life, I mean.

Once again I say to you: If you take one step towards God, be assured that God would take ten, maybe even a hundred steps towards you!

Arjuna, God is not interested in the **QUANTITY** of effort you put in; He is interested only in the **QUALITY** of your effort, and the **INTENSITY** of your faith.

ARJUNA: Krishna, now wait a minute please. When You

say You will bear all the burden of that person's welfare, will You also cancel karmic debts?

KRISHNA: Why not? That is where God's Grace comes in. Pleased with your faith and the sincerity of your effort, God might even cancel what is left of your karmic debt in one go. All you have to do is to love Him steadfastly.

ARJUNA: Krishna, I see a problem there.

KRISHNA: Which is?

ARJUNA: You say that man must love God. But is that not also attachment?

KRISHNA: [laughs] What a question!

**The *Gita* is often described as the quintessence of the *Upanishads*. That is indeed the case, but the *Gita* contains something that none of the *Upanishads* do, and that is a direct assurance from God to man. That guarantee can be given only by God and He did it for the first time on the battlefield in Kurukshetra more than five thousand years ago. That one eternal assurance alone makes the *Gita* priceless!**

Chapter 15

# HOW GOD IS IMMANENT IN CREATION, PROVIDING A LINK BETWEEN EVERYTHING

**Krishna introduces Arjuna to many ideas in this Chapter. The first is about how an uncontrolled Mind makes humans into slaves, and the next is about how God pervades the entire Universe. The key point is that God being immanent in the Universe, He can only be experienced and cannot be "seen". That is to say, His presence cannot be detected by the senses or even complex instruments, since scientific instruments are but mere extensions of the senses.**

KRISHNA: Arjuna, so you want to know why loving God does not amount to attachment. Obviously, you have not quite absorbed what I told you earlier about attachment, and this clearly means I have to repeat some of the basics. I explained then that man must not get attached to things of this **TRANSIENT WORLD**. Furthermore, God is **NOT** of this world. He is **ABOVE** and **BEYOND** this world. Hence, Love for God **DOES NOT** and **CANNOT** come in the category of worldly attachment!

ARJUNA: But Krishna, I still have a problem.

You are God, and right now You are here in this world along with me! I love You, which means

I love God. Frankly, I am getting confused. Are You here or up there or in both places? If You are here on earth and I love you, it still does not become attachment! How is that?

I am sorry I am giving You trouble, but Krishna please, have pity on me!

KRISHNA: [laughs] I think I understand your difficulty.

You and I are here now on earth, which is a part of the Universe. Before Creation, there was only God and nothing but God. That aspect of God is Formless and Nameless, and it is what may be called Unmanifest Divinity. This is the Supremest State of the Lord, and in this State, God is described as *Niraakara Brahman.*

ARJUNA: You mean to say God exists all by Himself, even when there is no Creation, no Universe?

KRISHNA: That is right; even when there is no Universe, God still exists; that is why He is called Eternal. He is truly beyond both Space and Time.

And when, God so willed, the Universe promptly came into existence. At first, there was only Space and Time; but soon God filled the Universe, first with inert matter, and then with living beings, starting from the lowliest species all the way to humans. Since the entire Universe came from God, the Divine aspect of God pervades the **ENTIRE** Universe, every bit of it, without any exception whatsoever.

Arjuna, now listen to this carefully. In this Universe, you might see many different things. The Universe is no doubt full of diversity, but every bit of this diversity rests on Me. Therefore, **EVERYTHING** in the Universe has the Divine aspect, and that includes you too!

The Universe may be called Manifest Divinity because it consists of objects created by God that are visible; however, God Himeslf is not directly visible. In the physical Universe, God cannot be seen with normal eyes because He is immanent; nevertheless, His presence can be easily inferred.

Arjuna, My power pervades every aspect of the Universe, whether it is big or small. That is why the *Vedas* describe God as *Anoraneeyaan, Mahatomahiyan,* that is to say, God is present everywhere, from the smallest of the small all the way to the largest of the large.

ARJUNA: Krishna, let me get this right; You are present in all entities, both animate and inanimate, and all the time, right?

KRISHNA: Absolutely; as I just told you, I am immanent in the atom **AND** in the Cosmos. I am immanent in the ant **AND** in the elephant. You name it, and I am there.

ARJUNA: You say You are everywhere; in that case, why is it we are not able to see God in all the various entities?

KRISHNA: This is a foolish question. Did I not tell you that I am immanent and not directly visible? That is why people miss Me.

ARJUNA: Can You make that a bit clearer please?

KRISHNA: Sure. Let us say you are walking on the road and you hear music coming from a house. Someone inside is singing and all you can hear is the song. Yet, do you doubt that there is a person behind that song? Then why this doubt about Me being behind everything?

ARJUNA: But Krishna, this is different. We know the connection between the song and singer. In the case of the Universe, where is the connection between say the ant and You, or the mountain and You, and so on?

KRISHNA: There **IS** a connection between the Creator and everything in Creation, but the problem is you are not making any effort to **UNDERSTAND** or **APPRECIATE** that connection.

ARJUNA: And what exactly is that connection?

KRISHNA: It is this way Arjuna: First of all you must know that I am not only the Creator but in fact the Ultimate. There is nothing beyond Me!! Remember that.

Since I am the Primordial Seed from which the entire Universe came into being, I automatically pervade everything that you can think of. I am, for example, present in all the five elements–sky, air, fire, water and earth.

You know how much power the oceans exhibit during a storm. Where does that power come from? From Me, because I am immanent in both water and in wind. And so on it goes, whether you are talking about the power of an earthquake, or of a volcano or whatever.

ARJUNA: [slowly] I see; I am beginning to get the picture.

KRISHNA: Yes Arjuna, I am present in all the five elements but to describe Me merely as present in this or that is only a limited way of looking at things. It is more appropriate to say that God **IS** the sky or the ether, God **IS** air, God **IS** fire and so on. In fact, everything in the Universe **IS** God, and truly speaking, there is nothing but God!

ARJUNA: That is amazing!

KRISHNA: Arjuna, you must have seen sages performing *Yajnas,* making offerings to the sacred fire and all that.

ARJUNA: Yes, I have seen those rituals being performed a few times. In fact, remember You came to one such *Yajna,* the *Rajasuya Yajna* performed by my eldest brother Dharmaputra?

KRISHNA: Yes, I do recall that event. Now let Me ask you: Do you understand the inner significance of what goes on during a *Yajna?*

ARJUNA: Krishna, how can I, a mere soldier, know all those things?

KRISHNA: Well, in that case listen closely, for I shall explain it all.

Arjuna, *Yajna* is a beautiful example of what I might call the complete Divine Cycle!

ARJUNA: Divine Cycle? What is that?

KRISHNA: Arjuna, during a *Yajna,* an offering is made; that act of offering is itself God!

ARJUNA: Amazing! Action itself becomes God!

KRISHNA: There is more; the one who makes the offering is not a priest but God Himself, playing the role of a priest in His Cosmic Drama. There is still more; that which is offered is God; the fire to which the offering is formally made is also God. And finally, the One who receives the offering is also God!

ARJUNA: This is incredible!

KRISHNA: Arjuna, there is nothing unique about the *Yajna.* If you look around, almost everywhere you would find the Divine Cycle in operation in some form or the other, all the time!

ARJUNA: And I suppose You would say that all this is a part of Your continuous and inscrutable Divine Drama?

KRISHNA: Indeed I would!

ARJUNA: But Krishna, why all this?

KRISHNA: Arjuna, did I not tell you earlier that you should stop questioning why God does this or that? When you act in a drama, you don't ask why the playwright wrote the script the way he did; you simply act, don't you?

ARJUNA: Yes, that is indeed true.

KRISHNA: In that case, why raise questions here? Why don't people simply obey God's commands, especially when it would benefit them so much?

ARJUNA: You have a point there!

Krishna, is it that people fail to see You in the Universe because they are not tuned to You?

KRISHNA: That is correct. Further, God teases man by hiding Himself. It is a game He likes to play!

ARJUNA: In what way does God hide Himself?

KRISHNA: Well, consider a garland with many beautiful flowers. Can a bunch of flowers form a garland all by themselves? You need a connecting thread, don't you? In fact, you also need a gardener who grows the flowers and someone who makes the garland. Yet, when you see a garland all by itself, are the connecting thread, the gardener, and the one who made the garland, visible to you?

ARJUNA: No!

KRISHNA: Well, it is the same thing here. Like the gardener,

I am the Creator of the Universe; and like the connecting thread, I am the foundation and the basis for everything present in the Universe. Can you have a house without a foundation? It is the same thing here; and like the foundation of a house, I remain hidden! Because I cannot be seen, people jump to the conclusion that I do not exist! How strange!

However, this does **NOT** mean My presence **CANNOT** be felt or experienced.

ARJUNA: What are the ways in which Your presence can be experienced?

KRISHNA: Here is an example; let us say you are very thirsty and your throat is absolutely parched. You see a clear stream with cool water flowing in it. You drink that water to your heart's content and find it very refreshing. But you do not know that the sweetness of that cool and fresh water is Me! It is I, latent as sweetness in that water, that brings joy to you.

Another example. It is a hot and humid day and you are perspiring heavily. Suddenly there is a gust of cool breeze and you feel relief. Arjuna, I am that breeze, giving you that refreshing experience.

ARJUNA: Amazing! You are everywhere, calling out to us all the time, and yet we miss you every time. Pretty dumb of us, I should say!

KRISHNA: No comments! But let me tell you my dear friend, that the Glory of God is everywhere to be seen, if only you would care to look.

I am the glory of a beautiful sunset, the radiant blue of the sky, and brilliance of the blazing fire. I am the beauty of a peacock as also the grace of a swan.

And so on it goes; the list is endless. Time being short, I won't give more examples, though I can go on and on! It is enough for you to know that all the excellence and beauty in the Universe flow directly from Me. If you see a very intelligent person, know for certain that this person's intelligence is not his own but flows from Me. Your brother Bhima is very strong; do you know that his strength is really a tiny part of My strength, reflected via him?

ARJUNA: Krishna, You have said many things I had never heard before. I really must take time to digest all that, and that clearly cannot be now. But meanwhile, there is one thing I am very eager to know.

KRISHNA: What is that?

ARJUNA: Well, if You are present everywhere and in everything, then are You present in me also?

KRISHNA: Of course, and in fact in three different ways.

ARJUNA: In three different ways? I do not follow.

KRISHNA: I shall explain.

**The description of immanence of God is not over. From the general, Krishna now takes the discussion to the specific, namely, how exactly is God present in every single individual. That is the subject of the next Chapter.**

Chapter 16

# THE VARIOUS WAYS IN WHICH GOD IS PRESENT IN HUMANS

**Having explained briefly how God is immanent in all entities in Creation, Krishna now describes the different ways in which God is present in humans. Krishna then explains how, while all entities in Creation except humans are hard-wired to function according to the Divine Master Plan, humans alone are given a Mind that has freedom of choice where action is concerned. This, Krishna explains, is really a test or an "entrance exam" for humans, intended to assess their eligibility for merger with God!**

KRISHNA: Arjuna, God is present everywhere, in everything, and in many different ways. In humans, I am present at three different levels; firstly the gross level, then at the subtle level and finally at the Causal level.

ARJUNA: What does that mean?

KRISHNA: Very simple. You have a body that is gross. What is it made up of? Of the five elements. I told you earlier that I am the five elements, which automatically means I am in every bit of your gross body, right?

ARJUNA: I follow that but can You tell me about the subtle presence?

KRISHNA: That is not difficult to understand either. You are a living being. What is the difference between a living being and a corpse? You know the answer to that, don't you? It is life, which is a subtle and most mysterious force. **I AM THAT MYSTERIOUS FORCE,** called *Praana Shakti.*

It is *Praana Shakti* that is able to make your body and the organs in it do so many things. You eat food which is later digested. How does that happen?

People say, "Oh that is all Nature. The stomach and the intestines do that work." All that is at the superficial level. In reality, it is **I WHO REALLY DIGESTS THAT FOOD,** as indeed I do in the case of all beings, irrespective of how they take in their food.

ARJUNA: What about the third level?

KRISHNA: The third level is a Causal one.

ARJUNA: And what does that mean?

KRISHNA: It means that I am present in you as the *Atma,* the Primordial Source from which everything came. Remember, **I AM THE *ATMA!***

ARJUNA: Are You present as the *Atma* in the ant also?

KRISHNA: Yes of course, but in You, I play a much higher role!

ARJUNA: What is that?

KRISHNA: Being aware of that higher role is Real Knowledge, and now we are coming to the core of My teaching to you!

ARJUNA: That's real nice, Krishna; I am very eager to know about the role played by the *Atma* in the various beings.

KRISHNA: Yes Arjuna, it is very important to know that. As I just told you, God and *Atma* are the same. Not only has everything come from the *Atma,* but in addition, the *Atma* is present in all. If the word *Atma* frightens you, then just take it that God is in all.

Now although the *Atma* is present in all entities, both animate and inanimate, it reveals its presence in different ways. In inanimate entities like a stone, for example, the *Atma* plays a passive role.

In living beings, the *Atma* plays two roles, as a passive entity as well as an active aspect called *Praana Shakti.* When the living being dies, the active aspect ceases–that is when we say the *Praana* is gone; after that, only the "passive" aspect of the *Atma* remains, since the body is dead and inert.

ARJUNA: Any other role that the *Atma* plays?

KRISHNA: Yes, in humans, there is a third role for the *Atma.*

ARJUNA: Which is?

KRISHNA: In humans, the *Atma* enables them to recognise the existence of God, both outside and within. It is the *Atma* that enables humans to be both conscious [of the external world] and recognise the existence of Conscience or God within.

Once a person becomes aware that God is within, then slowly that person's life begins to be shaped and guided by the *Atma,* and that is how the human slowly rises to the level of God.

ARJUNA: Krishna, what exactly do you mean by saying humans rise to the level of God?

KRISHNA: That is simple; what I mean is that humans become more and more pure.

ARJUNA: How do I know I am becoming more and more pure?

KRISHNA: That also is simple. Now what are the impurities contaminating the Godliness in you? Desire, selfishness, anger, jealousy, etc. If these traits are progressively reduced, then automatically your purity increases.

ARJUNA: In practical terms, what does that mean?

KRISHNA: It means your feelings, thoughts, words and actions must all be in harmony and free from contamination. Arjuna, **thought, words and deed must always be pure and in total in harmony with each other.** This is called *Trikarana Suddhi,* and is very important.

ARJUNA: Krishna, I want to go back to something we were discussing earlier. You say that God is Formless; but right now, You are here before me with a very beautiful Form! I am confused. Are You Formless at times and have a Form at other times?

KRISHNA: That is an interesting question! God is Eternal, Formless and always exists. This aspect of God is referred to as *Niraakara Brahman.* As I told you before, that aspect of God **ALWAYS EXISTS, WHETHER OR NOT THERE IS A UNIVERSE.**

ARJUNA: Krishna, You say that even after Creation, God continues to exist as the Formless God or *Niraakaara Brahman.* But You also say that God is immanent in the Universe in a million different ways. How come?

KRISHNA: [laughs] Arjuna, you seem to have a dim view of God's power and abilities. Let Me tell you something: God can exist simultaneously, as *Niraakara Brahman* at a level **beyond Space and Time, and also as the Immanent God in Creation, that is below Space and Time.**

ARJUNA: [shakes his head and says] Bit too heavy for me! Can You make it simpler please?

KRISHNA: [smiles] I shall. First of all, you understand, don't you that God always exists as *Niraakaara Brahman* or the Formless God, beyond Space and Time? You agree with that?

ARJUNA: [slowly] I think I do.

KRISHNA: Good. Now one fine day, this Formless God wills that there shall be a Universe; *presto,* and the Universe is born. You follow that also, I presume.

ARJUNA: Yes.

KRISHNA: I am glad we are making progress! Now in the Universe that has been created, God becomes immanent in every entity, from the atom and the ant to the clouds and the Cosmos itself–agreed?

ARJUNA: Yes; by the way, is this what the *Vedas* refer to as the ONE becoming Many?

KRISHNA: Exactly. And Arjuna, please note that the entities in Creation have names and very often forms too.

ARJUNA: And I suppose that these forms include the beautiful one before me–right?

KRISHNA: [smiles] Indeed!

ARJUNA: Krishna, does that mean that when You assume

a distinct form, God ceases to be *Niraakara Brahman?*

KRISHNA: No, no Arjuna! You seem to have completely forgotten something I told you just a short while ago!! God **ALWAYS** exists as the Formless God or *Niraakara Brahman;* that aspect goes on for ever, non-stop.

ARJUNA: In which case, the human form of God is very special–is that it?

KRISHNA: Absolutely! Remember what I said earlier about water vapour and clouds? *Niraakara Brahman* is like the water vapour–not visible; and He always is. Just as occasionally water vapour manifests as a cloud, the Formless God occasionally makes His appearance on earth bearing a human form. While *Niraakara Brahman* is invisible, when He incarnates with a Form, He obviously becomes visible. An incarnation of God is called an *Avatar.*

ARJUNA: Any special name for *Brahman* when He incarnates with a form like You have now?

KRISHNA: There sure is.

ARJUNA: And that name is?

KRISHNA: It is *Saakara Brahman.*

ARJUNA: Let me see if I have got all that You said so far:

God without Form is called *Niraakaara Brahman*. He always is, whether there is a Universe or not. Next, when He creates a Universe, God becomes immanent in every single entity in the Universe; that is how the power of God becomes embedded in everything from the atom upwards. While God is immanent in Creation, it does not mean He ceases to be *Niraakaara Brahman*–that aspect is ever in existence; **IT ALWAYS IS**. Thus, God exists simultaneously at two levels–one is **BEYOND** Space and Time, while the other is **BELOW** Space and Time. And in the latter aspect, when God appears with a special Form like You bear now, He is called *Saakaara Brahman?* Right so far?

KRISHNA: Brilliant!

ARJUNA: O Krishna, I am so relieved to hear that!

KRISHNA: Any more doubts to be cleared or clarifications you want?

ARJUNA: Yes; God being immanent all over, I suppose that every entity in the Creation is God with a particular Form. Thus, wind is God, fire is God, mountain is God and so forth; am I getting it correct?

KRISHNA: You are.

ARJUNA: All right, now please tell me O Lord, what exactly does God do after creating the Universe?

In other words, I want to know something about God's *Leela* in ordaining Creation.

KRISHNA: He just watches to see what the entities in Creation are doing.

ARJUNA: What are these entities supposed to do?

KRISHNA: That I told you earlier. Basically, every entity is supposed to play a role in My Drama according to some rules.

ARJUNA: But Krishna, what about inanimate entities like stone? How can they know anything about rules when even humans often do not?

KRISHNA: Good question. Inanimate entities are ordained by Me to automatically do what they are supposed to. A stone has no active consciousness. Nevertheless, a stone knows what to do when dropped; it just falls to the ground. Man sees this happening all the time and calls it Laws of Nature. I call it the *Dharma* of inanimate entities in Nature.

ARJUNA: Krishna, I understand what You say about inanimate entities like stones. What about living things like birds, animals and so on?

KRISHNA: They too have a *Dharma* of their own; once again, they do exactly as God ordained them to do. Take a cat, for example. When it gives birth to kitten, the mother cat is very protective of the kitten.

ARJUNA: But that is the motherly instinct, is it not?

KRISHNA: Where did that so-called motherly instinct come from?

ARJUNA: It is natural! It is just there, built into the mother cat!

KRISHNA: That is how foolish people try to appear intelligent! I will tell you wherefrom that protective instinct comes. From Me!

ARJUNA: Came from You? What has Divinity got to do with a cat and her kitten?

KRISHNA: Arjuna, for you it is just a cat and her kitten but for Me it is something else. I am in the mother cat and also in the little kitten. What you see as the mother protecting her babies is really Me loving Myself! Don't you understand? It is one aspect of Me in Creation, loving another aspect of Myself in Creation!

ARJUNA: Sounds a bit complicated to me! Krishna, please, would You go over once more about this strange drama going on in Creation?

KRISHNA: Sure. Arjuna, in a nutshell, all that you see in this world are really different forms of Me acting in different roles!

ARJUNA: But why on earth do You want to do that?

KRISHNA: Because this is a game I play.

ARJUNA: You, the Lord of the Universe, playing a game? This is unbelievable!

KRISHNA: There is nothing strange about it, and I explained it earlier.

My game is like the mono-act type of play that you humans stage sometimes. Mine is also a mono-act of a kind but **IMMENSE** in scope. The unique thing about My play is that all the different characters are visible at the same time; but inside each, I am there!

ARJUNA: Krishna, what is the purpose of this strange game?

KRISHNA: Do you remember what I told you earlier, namely that for Love to manifest, a platform is needed? That platform is the Universe and the animate entities in Creation represent different aspects of Me involved in the playacting. In this game or play of Mine, every form of Myself is supposed to show Love for every other Form. However, that does not happen in practice!

ARJUNA: That I am able to see; otherwise, how could we have all this hatred that we see around? But then, why do not the different forms Love each other?

KRISHNA: Ah, that happens because of the influence of the *gunas*.

ARJUNA: And *gunas* are shaped to a large extent by the forces of the world?

KRISHNA: Sure. People become greedy. About what? About the many things they see in the external world. They are tempted by this and that, and want to have all of them. They fail to realise that the moment they die their possessions mean nothing. Greed arises on account of giving importance to the transient. However, if their focus is on the *Atma,* then there would be no problem.

ARJUNA: Krishna, when people forget to Love each other, does that not mean that Your play is being ruined?

KRISHNA: Not exactly; what happens is that the play becomes more interesting.

ARJUNA: In what way?

KRISHNA: It gives Me a chance to incarnate with a human form and move with people like you! Otherwise, do you think I would be here?

ARJUNA: I never thought of that! Krishna, let me now turn to something we have not discussed thus far.

KRISHNA: And that is?

ARJUNA: Well, when and why does God, the Formless, incarnate?

KRISHNA: Ah, that is an important question and it merits a detailed answer.

**Basically, what Krishna has done in this Chapter is to explain further certain nuances of His Divine Drama in which all of us humans are actors. People often ask: "Is everything pre-ordained? If that is so, even the mistakes and the sins we commit are; in which case, why should there be a Law of *Karma* and punishment arising thereof?" This issue is better understood if we regard life as an "examination". If the candidate, i.e., humans, give the "right answers" [meaning they act in accordance with *Dharma*], they pass; otherwise, they have to "repeat" by taking a new birth. In this sense, the examination is pre-ordained for sure, but in as much the Mind has the freedom "to find answers to issues and problems" the way it wants, success or failure are really in our hands. The good news is that if we are determined to pass, then God is ready to help by acting as our "coach"; but like every teacher, He may coach till the last minute before the test, but during the exam itself, He would just watch! That is precisely what happened in the Kurukshetra war too. Krishna instructed and then left the ultimate decision (to fight or not to fight) to Arjuna. Luckily, Arjuna made the right choice and he was redeemed!**

Chapter 17

# GOD AS THE PRODUCER AND DIRECTOR OF THE DIVINE DRAMA

**It is interesting to see how far the discussion has moved away from war and fighting! That is because Krishna's teachings are NOT about war and fighting but about how humans should perform their duty, in the situation in which Destiny places them in. Duty as God wants us to perform it cannot be done in a robotic fashion, and it requires a thorough understanding of many things; it is precisely those matters that the Lord is now explaining. Thus, in this Chapter, attention is focussed on two topics: 1) Why and when God comes down as an *Avatar*, and 2) do humans have freewill [as they often imagine they do], or do they not?**

KRISHNA: Arjuna, you have asked an important question about when and why God incarnates on earth, and that merits a detailed answer.

You see Arjuna, God, in His Formless aspect, ordains Creation, lays down rules according to which entities in Creation would function, and after that He just watches what is going on. In other words, once the Universe has been set in motion, God functions largely as a Witness.

ARJUNA: But Krishna, I thought You were involved in a Divine Mono-act. One minute You are saying that You are doing the acting and the next minute You say that You are merely a passive witness–all this is very confusing!

KRISHNA: Arjuna, the problem is with you and not with Me. How can you learn anything if you are so impatient? In fact, impatience is responsible for so many of mankind's problems.

ARJUNA: Sorry about that!

KRISHNA: I hope this would be the last time you try to get away simply by saying sorry! Now let Me get back to what I was saying.

All entities in Creation are supposed to follow certain rules. Inanimate entities follow what some scholars refer to as the Laws of Nature. Animals and birds function according to what is commonly described as pure instinct. As I told you earlier, the Laws of Nature as well as the so-called instincts, both come from Me!

In short, where the inanimate entities and living species other than humans are concerned, things run pretty much as ordained by Me!

However, when it comes to human beings, it is a different story; things do not happen automatically.

ARJUNA: Why is that?

KRISHNA: Because of the Mind! While animals follow pre-ordained natural instincts, man acts in the way his Mind tells him to. It is man who decides what his actions would be, and that happens because of the power of decision-making endowed by God to the Mind.

Take your own case. Earlier, you were dead set on fighting the Kauravas. But here on the battlefield, your Mind, monkey mind if I may say so, deluded you and made you say, "No, I will not fight!"

ARJUNA: Krishna, are You saying that humans have what is often called freewill? That is to say, humans can decide on how they would act under any given situation? And that it is this flexibility of the Mind that is responsible for Your Divine Play going off the rails sometimes?

KRISHNA: Yes, it is the flexibility of the Mind that leads to all kinds of problems.

ARJUNA: Krishna, in that case, why did You give humans the gift of freewill?

KRISHNA: That is an important question, because it touches upon a few critical issues; but first, let Me get back to the question of when and why God appears on earth with a Form; you will recall that I have not yet completed the answer to that question.

Arjuna, as I told you earlier, God is Love, and Compassion is one of the manifestations of Love. When God finds that His children are in deep trouble because they have lost their way in their return journey to God, He comes down in human form to help directly and in person. And let Me repeat that humans get into trouble largely because, in the name of so-called freewill, they misuse their Minds.

ARJUNA: Seeing the way You are helping me right now, I am beginning to get that point. But Krishna, in general, what are the ways in which God helps when He comes down as an *Avatar?*

KRISHNA: Oh, there are so many ways, too numerous to mention right now; remember, the fighting is all set to start. However, since you have asked, let Me briefly say this.

Donning a Human Form, I come down from My Formless and Higher Aspect, for two main reasons. First is to protect My devotees, and the second is to help *Dharma* get re-established in all its glory. I do this in many ways, one of them being the elimination of people who try to destabilise *Dharma* in a massive way. In general, God comes down as man to help man rise to the level of God–that is the basic reason behind every incarnation.

ARJUNA: Krishna, people say that when God incarnates, He annihilates the evildoers, and that is how He re-establishes *Dharma.* Does God always have to engage in annihilation for re-establishing *Dharma?*

KRISHNA: No Arjuna, the *Avatar* does not always resort to extermination and annihilation, as many seem to imagine. Yes, in some of the earlier incarnations, that was the strategy that was adopted. However, there are also other methods that God in human form uses. In general, the *Avatar* helps in the restoration of *Dharma* in various ways; use of weapons to eliminate the wicked is just one of the many methods employed by the *Avatar*.

ARJUNA: Can you please elaborate a bit on that last part?

KRISHNA: Sure. You can easily see that when the population of the world is very large and *adharma* is widespread, one cannot resort to annihilation; that would merely lead to a bloodbath. Clearly, other methods have to be used, and the most important of these is **transformation**; maybe I shall discuss that later. For the present, it is enough for you to know that I occasionally incarnate to play a role in My own Drama. By the way, many of these subtleties are not known even to the *Devas* or the demi-gods.

ARJUNA: Krishna, before You take me any further, can I get back to the freewill business please? I have some doubts there.

KRISHNA: As you wish.

ARJUNA: Very well then. As I was trying to ask earlier, when God created humans, He must have known for sure that their Minds, monkey minds as You refer to them, would, in the name of freewill, make them get into all sorts of troubles. So my question is: "Knowing all this very well, why did God ordain things in such a manner that there was more than a 90 % chance for humans to get into problems?" That does not look very fair to me!

KRISHNA: Arjuna, your very question illustrates why humans get into trouble. The problem with you humans is that though you have a very fertile brain–God-given brain I might add–where Spiritual matters are concerned, you have stopped thinking deeply and analysing matters thoroughly.

ARJUNA: Why do You say that?

KRISHNA: Well, let us start with the word freewill that you humans tend to use so glibly. Tell me Arjuna, when is a thing said to be free?

ARJUNA: Let me see–is it correct to say a thing is free when there is no price to pay for it?

KRISHNA: That's exactly right. Let us take gambling. You ought to know very well how gambling can ruin a person! Consider a person who is tempted to engage in gambling. Suppose the King has banned gambling; what do those who want to gamble do? Some of them try and gamble secretly; others protest, claiming that they have a right to gamble, etc. If anyone tries to advise and says, "Look, gambling is bad," these addicts retort, "Maybe, but each individual should have the right to decide that," and so on. And when, in this manner, people do things that are not necessarily good for them, in defiance of their Conscience, they try to justify it all in the name of freewill.

Tell Me Arjuna, isn't that what happens almost invariably?

ARJUNA: Yes.

KRISHNA: I am glad you agree. Now, let us see what is free about this so-called exercise of freewill. Arjuna, I have told you many things; keeping all those things in Mind, tell Me, why do people get attracted to gambling, drinking, etc.?

ARJUNA: I believe they are drawn to these dangerous acts by the sense-Mind combination that drags them into the external world.

KRISHNA: Wonderful; you are right on track, and My congratulations!

Arjuna, just recall the words you have used–you said that the senses and the Mind drag the person into the external world and get him or her stuck in a quagmire. These words automatically imply that the Mind and the senses are not free! Rather, they are slaves; and to what are they slaves? Can you answer that?

ARJUNA: I think I can; I believe they are slaves to desires–am I right?

KRISHNA: On the dot and congratulations again. So, do you see that you have answered your own question? How can humans claim that they are acting according to their freewill, when almost invariably all such actions are the result of bondage to desire, anger, jealousy, etc.? It is like a slave claiming to be free! Do you follow Arjuna, do you see the irony of it all?

ARJUNA: [slowly] Krishna, I think I do. You said that if a thing is truly free, there is no price to pay. I presume that when one becomes a slave to the internal enemies, the price tag is karmic debt; am I getting it right?

KRISHNA: Absolutely; people may delude themselves that they are acting out of freewill, when, in fact, they are slaves; and those actions, which they believe are the result of freewill, **ALWAYS** have a price tag!

ARJUNA: Krishna, does that mean no one has freewill?

KRISHNA: Actually, there is One who has it!

ARJUNA: And who is that?

KRISHNA: Can you not guess? God, of course! He alone is free from karmic debt. When humans are born, it is the result of actions of earlier births or *janmas.* But when God comes down in human form, it is entirely the result of His own Freewill. He decides when He would so come, where exactly He would make His appearance, who His bodily parents would be, the time of His appearance, how long He would stay, and so on. Since it is all a part of the Divine Play of the Lord, His incarnation is sometimes referred to as *Leela Janma.*

ARJUNA: [slowly] I see. From what You say, docs it mean that when man merges with God, he has freewill?

KRISHNA: Arjuna, you must understand that when man merges with God there is only One and **not** two! So, do not talk as if man has separate existence. At that point where merger is truly complete, there is only God, the identity of the other person having been totally subsumed in God!

ARJUNA: That is a bit tough for me to grasp right away but nevertheless, I shall accept what You say. But right now, let me ask the other question regarding the Mind going astray and all that.

KRISHNA: What is that other question that is bothering you?

ARJUNA: Krishna, God knows everything. That being the case, why did God, who is so compassionate, give humans a Mind that could easily be seduced, dragged into problems, etc.? Is that not unfair?

KRISHNA: You are forgetting that God also gave man a

Conscience that would help him to be on track. Why blame God when man insists on being stupid?

ARJUNA: But Krishna, even so, could You not have been a bit more compassionate and saved man some trouble?

KRISHNA: Listen, is it not a fact that humans are ready to overcome enormous obstacles in order to achieve something substantial in this word? Take your own case; you became a famous archer; did that happen like magic? Did you not practice hard and persevere in order to become the very best?

ARJUNA: I agree that human achievement comes only after great effort, but what exactly is the point You are making?

KRISHNA: Arjuna, you have to understand that life is a kind of a continuous examination conducted by God. As you act, accounts are kept of the way you make decisions, guided by your Mind. If you act on the side of *Dharma,* you get positive marks; but if, misguided by your Mind you support *adharma,* you get negative marks.

ARJUNA: But Krishna, why should God conduct this exam?

KRISHNA: In this world, do they not hold competitions and decide on winners? Have you not won such competitions yourself? It is the same with God; He wants humans to prove their eligibility for permanent merger with Him! That is all! Why do you complain when there is an entrance test to Heaven, while you people have so many qualifying tests here on earth?

ARJUNA: But this is different.

KRISHNA: In what way?

ARJUNA: Come on Krishna, don't you know that the Mind is so difficult to control?

KRISHNA: Yes it is, but most humans try to quit even before trying. Others have done it and so why can't you? You just don't want to try, that is all!

ARJUNA: No Krishna, You are trying to make it sound all so very simple, and You know it is not!

KRISHNA: Arjuna, listen to Me carefully. Life has been given so that you come back permanently to your **REAL** home. God wants you to, and He is ever ready to help. The trick is to have deep faith in God and try your best. If you do that, be assured you would be helped in plenty!

Come on, let us move to other matters. What more do you wish to know about?

**Having been exposed to *Atma Vidya* for the first time, Arjuna is not through yet, and has many doubts still. Let us move on and see what is the next topic on which God would be conversing with man!**

Chapter 18

# EVERYTHING IS GOD AND THERE IS NOTHING BUT GOD

**Slowly, the conversation is moving towards the Cosmic Omnipresence and Omnipotence of the Lord, and, as a prelude, Krishna first explains that apart from His manifestations via beauty in Nature, God reveals Himself even more wonderfully via various virtues, especially compassion and fortitude. Let us join Krishna and Arjuna to learn about all that.**

ARJUNA: Krishna, I am able to vaguely understand that as the Immanent God, You are present everywhere and in everything in this Universe, but are **not** visible to the normal eye. How then am I to recognise Your subtle presence, Your immanence? Can You give me some practical tips?

KRISHNA: Sure. Whenever you see goodness, recognise that goodness to be a signature of the Divine. When a man is good, the Divinity in him automatically shines via various virtues. All virtues, like *Kshama* or forbearance, for example, are manifestations of God.

ARJUNA: Any other examples?

KRISHNA: Arjuna, do you realise there are innumerable manifestations of God in this Universe?

The beauty of a peacock is God. The glory of a

sunset is God. The majesty of mountains is God. **Everything is God.** Yet, people complain they cannot see God. How strange!

ARJUNA: Yes Krishna, it is indeed very strange but then, why does this inability to experience the immanence of God arise in the first place?

KRISHNA: In simple language, people whose *Buddhi* is sharp have no difficulty at all in seeing Me and experiencing My Glory everywhere! Believe Me, wherever they turn they see only Me and nothing else!

ARJUNA: So this inability to experience the Omnipresence of God is due to *Buddhi* becoming blunt, and people losing the ability for Fundamental Discrimination–is that it?

KRISHNA: Correct.

ARJUNA: Krishna, You are telling me wonderful things I did not know until now. I am now filled with a deep desire to know more about You! Please O Lord, would You most kindly tell me all You can about Your Glory and Grandeur?

KRISHNA: Arjuna, My Glories are literally infinite, and right now, we have very little time; so I can give you only the barest glimpse. Later, you can contemplate in leisure on My Limitless and Incomparable Glory and Grandeur.

ARJUNA: I am grateful to You my Lord for granting my request!

KRISHNA: Arjuna, since I pervade everything, My Glory also is spread everywhere. Anything beautiful, grand, wondrous, magnificent, and marvellous that you see in Creation is just Me greeting you via that channel!

It can be anything–a starry sky, a majestic mountain, a roaring waterfall, a mighty river or even a gentle stream, a fabulous beach, the atolls, the coral reefs, the soaring birds, the coloured fishes, the royal tiger–all these are nothing but Me in various disguises, and the beauty that you see in these entities and admire, originates from Me!

I appear in diverse forms to make people happy in many different ways; do you understand, Arjuna?

ARJUNA: Honestly Lord, I understand only to a limited extent. How can Infinity be grasped in an instant?

KRISHNA: That is the excuse man often uses to postpone becoming one with God.

Arjuna, take it from Me, even Infinity can be attained in an instant, provided a **DEEP** yearning is there. However, I know human weaknesses, frailties and tendencies. Therefore, Arjuna, in whatever ways people seek Me, in that very same way do I respond. I am ever ready to oblige and give *Ananda* or Bliss to all those who seek it.

Can man ask for more? I go to the extent of saying, "O man, if only you would take one small step towards Me with Pure Love, I shall take a million and come to you in an instant!"

ARJUNA: Lord, that shows how much You love and care for Your children.

KRISHNA: I am glad you appreciate that; if only My children would show similar Love to Me! But then, these are times when children are slowly beginning to forget even their bodily parents! If they can be so ungrateful to the physical parents whom they have seen, how can they ever be grateful to the Supreme Parent whom they have not seen?

ARJUNA: O Lord, what can I say in response to that? All I can say is that with all our faults, You are so kind and forgiving.

KRISHNA: That is right Arjuna, Pure Love gives, forgives, and always forgets that it gave Selflessly.

ARJUNA: Lord, out of compassion for me, You have explained to me most clearly as to who exactly You are and how You pervade the entire Universe. As a result, I have a slightly better understanding of the immanence of God in the Universe.

And now, O Lord, most humbly and respectfully I make a request. Can I see You in Your mighty Cosmic Form please? Is it at all possible?

KRISHNA: Arjuna, you are asking to see what has rarely been seen before. For you, however, I shall make an exception and reveal My Cosmic Form. Get hold of yourself and be ready to see something that is not only breathtaking but also truly awesome!

**What happens next is an amazing scene, when Krishna specially endows Arjuna with the ability to behold the Cosmic Form of God. It is said that this was a vision specially granted to Arjuna so that through Arjuna, humanity itself would get a glimpse of the Omnipresence as well as the Infinite power of God. Arjuna, who obviously did not know what to expect, is completely overwhelmed when he beholds the Cosmic Expanse of the Lord.**

ARJUNA: Lord, I am at a loss for words! Within Your blazing Form I can see everything, every being and every entity in Creation. This incredible Form before me does not seem to have either a beginning or an end. Mind-boggling it truly is!

O my dearest Lord! I realise now, feebly perhaps, that You are at once the Eternal Being, the Supreme One, and the goal that is to be attained. Till now, I used to think that the fleeting and transient world was the Reality. I now realise how wrong I was, and that it is You alone who are truly the Ultimate Reality.

By You alone is filled the space between heaven and earth. O Almighty Lord, the three worlds tremble at the sight of Your wondrous but terrifying Form!

As I behold Your Supremely Effulgent Form

stretching to the very heavens, I am absolutely petrified and totally bewildered. I just cannot bear this overpowering vision.

I am terribly frightened because I see in You all that is expected to happen in the future, especially the death of our arch enemies.

As the moths fly into the flame only to be destroyed, I see these people plunging into Destiny to meet their violent end.

Tell me O Lord, Who presents such an awesome Form that strikes me with mortal fear and fills me with infinite dread, tell me O Lord, Who exactly are You?

KRISHNA: Arjuna, I am **TIME,** and to Me as **TIME,** everything in Creation **HAS** to bow!

I am Destiny, and I have destined death for every creature that is born. In this transient world that I have created, there is no physical immortality. All, including those whom you are hesitant to slay, will die, whether you slay them or not.

Arjuna, when the bodies of all these people are doomed to perish, why do you hesitate to engage them in battle, especially when **I am ordering you** to do so, and that too in the cause of *Dharma?*

Now that you have got a glimpse of Me as **TIME** and **DESTINY,** it behoves you to implicitly obey My command. Cast aside your doubts and misgivings, and trust Me. Place your faith in Me. Pick up your bow and arrows. Get up, and prepare to go out there and fight!

Arjuna, Creation is a Cosmic Drama, scripted, produced, directed and staged by Me for My pleasure. All beings are actors, nay puppets. Everyone is a puppet–a few know it but most do not.

Nothing can happen, unless it is according to My Will. Not even a blade of grass can move, unless I will that it be so. People do not understand this. You too! I have already ordained that Bhishma and Drona shall die in this war. And they will too for sure, whether you fight or not. The question is whether you want to accept the role I am giving you, or you want to quit.

Once again, I say to you: Get up and fight, and slay your enemies. Don't think you are killing them, for you are not. Rather, they are being swallowed by **TIME**. Performing your duty thinking of Me, you would be merely assisting and helping in the restoration of *Dharma.*

**Much has been written about the Cosmic Vision granted to Arjuna, including how Krishna gave Arjuna special powers for having that vision. Bhagavan Baba says, however, that it is all a question of linking everything seen in the**

Universe based on one single connecting thread, the thread of Divinity.

Everything that happens in the Universe is but a part of one single Cosmic Drama. However, on account of Spiritual ignorance or *ajnana,* we invariably see the Drama as a sequence of disjointed events and disconnected occurrences. Krishna temporarily disabled that *ajnana* in Arjuna, enabling him to see everything as parts of One Cosmic Drama staged by God.

Baba says anyone can achieve this Cosmic integration of vision and experience such a unified, all-encompassing oneness, once *ajnana* or Spiritual ignorance is overcome. Thus, the inner significance of the Cosmic Vision is that it is only by getting rid of *ajnana* that one can experience the Omnipresence of God, that is, see only God, in everything, everywhere, all the time! Baba refers to this as Constant Integrated Awareness.

Chapter 19

# THE DIFFERENCE BETWEEN MAN AND GOD

**Having offered a glimpse of His Cosmic Form, Krishna reverts back to His human form and the conversation continues as before, with Krishna explaining the basic difference between God in human form and ordinary mortals. Following that, some useful tips about how to be in the world and yet not be affected by it. As we rejoin Krishna and Arjuna, the latter is still beholding the awesome Cosmic Aspect of the Lord.**

KRISHNA: Arjuna, have you seen everything you yearned to? Are you happy, are you satisfied?

ARJUNA: Lord, I am literally speechless. Struggling for expression, let me say in all reverence that I now understand why devotees constantly chant Your Name and never miss an opportunity to proclaim Your matchless Glory.

And why not my Lord, since You are everything and there is nothing other than You?

Lord, at this point I have an apology to make. Till now, not knowing who exactly You are, I have taken many liberties with You, often imagining You to be merely Krishna, my friend.

Please pardon me my Lord, for all my

indiscretions. I feel extremely ashamed and also most embarrassed. I just don't know how to seek Your forgiveness. All I can say is: Please forgive me, and forget all that I said or did in stupidity and ignorance.

Prostrating before You, I pray to You to bear with me, even as a father is indulgent to his wayward son, and a kind man is to his errant friend.

As for this extra-ordinary vision that You have granted me, I rejoice that I have seen what no man has until now. At the same time, this spectacle is most awesome. Therefore, my Lord, I humbly pray that You revert to Your normal human form, the beautiful, ever-smiling form of Krishna, that we all are so accustomed to.

**At this point, Krishna reverts from His Cosmic to His human form, which puts Arjuna at ease. The conversation continues.**

KRISHNA: Arjuna, do you realise that you have seen what even *Rishis* and the *Devas* have not? This vision is a privilege that no austerity can ever earn; and yet, you have been blessed with that. Do you know why? Because you are dear to Me, that is why!

ARJUNA: How fortunate am I to hear from the Lord Himself that I am dear to Him!

KRISHNA: Arjuna, as a matter of fact all are dear to Me, for are they not all My children?

ARJUNA: O Lord, if only all of us would realise that!

KRISHNA: That's right Arjuna; if only man would realise that I am ever ready to help, assist and oblige in every possible way! All that he has to do is to follow My commands, and that would please Me no end. Soon I shall tell you how that can be done.

For now, understand that he who is steadfast in his devotion to Me, who dedicates every action of his to Me, who is free from worldly attachment–such a one would unfailingly come to Me.

[After a pause and with much concern] Arjuna, you continue to look pretty dazed; are you alright?

ARJUNA: Lord, what can I say! I came here with a friend and now I am with God!

KRISHNA: Arjuna, you seem to forget that God is in fact your best friend! Humans would be friendly to you as along as it suits them but let trouble visit you and these so-called friends would simply vanish! God is **NOT** like that; He **ALWAYS** helps and comes to your side even though all others might have abandoned you. He alone is your **TRUE** Friend!

ARJUNA: Lord, I want to go back to the question of Lord incarnating on earth. What is the difference between You the Formless God, and You the God with Form?

KRISHNA: That is a good question! I am Formless as the Unmanifest Divinity but when I incarnate, I take a Form, restricting Myself to many of the limitations that apply to humans. With a Form, this body of Mine has *Praana* or the Life Principle; and with that come automatically, certain limitations. I do not have to impose those restrictions on Myself but I do so for the sake of humanity.

ARJUNA: O Lord, You are so compassionate! Can I know something more about this Life Principle?

KRISHNA: Sure. This Life Principle is sometimes called *Jiva,* and is an aspect of Creation. My Unmanifest Divinity is the source of this *Jiva.*

Earlier I described a living person as the *Atma* "trapped" in a cage or the body. The embodied *Atma* or the Individualised Soul is also called the *Jivatma.* Thus, Arjuna, you are a *Jivatma.*

ARJUNA: Krishna what about You? Are You also a *Jivatma?*

KRISHNA: No way! I am special; I am the *Paramatma* or the Universal Soul!

ARJUNA: What is the difference between the *Paramatma* and the *Jivatma?*

KRISHNA: Well, the essential difference is that the *Jivatma* is wrapped up in *dehabhimaanam* or body-consciousness; the *Paramatma* is not.

ARJUNA: What happens as a result?

KRISHNA: Thanks to body-consciousness, the *Jivatma* does not quite realise that he or she is God. The day this veil of ignorance drops and the individual realises that there really is no difference between that person and God, the *Jivatma* rises to the level of the *Paramatma.*

ARJUNA: So, ignorance makes all the difference?

KRISHNA: Indeed it does. I am God and so are you; the difference is that while I **KNOW** that I am God, you do **NOT!**

ARJUNA: Krishna, how can You say that? You just told me I am God and I now know that fact.

KRISHNA: Knowing that in your head is different from **FEELING** that in your Heart!

ARJUNA: Say that again please?

KRISHNA: Arjuna, your tongue may say that you are God, but do you actually **FEEL** that, in your Heart? Do you, when you see all these diverse forms before you, experience an over-riding sense of Supreme Oneness that wipes out all the superficial differences, fusing everything into one Cosmic Entity?

ARJUNA: I am afraid I do not yet have that feeling.

KRISHNA: Well, that means that there is a lot of work ahead of you!

ARJUNA: Krishna, I am not able to see how one can ever

have this feeling of Cosmic Oneness that You are talking about. After all, both You and I are in this world that is so full of bewildering diversity. We just cannot wish it away. In fact, just a short while ago, You asked me to fight Bhishma, Drona and such others. If they are all God, how can I fight with God?!

KRISHNA: You know Arjuna, you can make even God get frustrated!

ARJUNA: I am very sorry, but Lord, please understand my pitiable situation! I am very eager to do what You command, but don't You think I should understand what You are asking me to do?

KRISHNA: You have a point there.

It is this way Arjuna. You have a Soul and you also have a body. So you must really function at two levels; and you must function in such a way that while your body reacts to diversity, the Soul does not!

ARJUNA: That is awfully confusing! What exactly do You mean?

KRISHNA: The answer to that is important, and so pay careful attention. Since humans are in this world–and remember God put them there–they sure have to function in this world; that is point number one.

Point number two: Destiny has put them there, and, as a result, circumstances might arise where one faces apparent Moral dilemmas. When this happens, one should not go around moping or complaining, "O God, why did You do this to me?" and so on. Instead, people must do their duty, as I instructed you earlier.

ARJUNA: You mean they must consult *Buddhi,* follow *Atma Dharma,* etc.?

KRISHNA: Correct.

ARJUNA: Fine, but where do the two levels You talked about, enter into the picture?

KRISHNA: Ah, I am coming precisely to that. The best way of answering your question is to recall an incident from My previous incarnation.

ARJUNA: You mean as Lord Sri Rama?

KRISHNA: That's right. You will recall that during that incarnation, there came a time when Rama had to wage war with Ravana.

ARJUNA: I remember that very well.

KRISHNA: Well, during that war, one day Ravana became very tired and was knocked out of his chariot. He fell down and was lying on the ground practically helpless. Do you know what happened then?

ARJUNA: I think I do; Rama asked Ravana go back home, take rest and come back refreshed the next day to resume the fighting.

KRISHNA: Arjuna, why do you think Rama did that? Why

did He not finish off Ravana then and there?

ARJUNA: You know Krishna, I have always wondered about that!

KRISHNA: No surprise you did; as a warrior, that precisely is what I expect you to do. However, Arjuna, Rama was no ordinary warrior; He was the very incarnation of God and God does things differently! That is what I want you to understand!

ARJUNA: Krishna, please do not keep me in suspense! Tell me why did Rama do something that mortals like me would not.

KRISHNA: I sure shall, and this is the point really. You see Arjuna, Rama was not engaged in war but in punishing Ravana for the latter's misdeeds. When He dealt with Ravana, there was no malice or hatred in Rama's Heart. How could there ever be?!

In other words, Rama was dealing with Ravana at two levels. At the level of the body, there was the punishment angle. At the level of the Heart, there was the feeling that Ravana must be corrected, helped and made to realise his mistake; in other words, there was really compassion.

ARJUNA: Let me see if I have got it right. Are You saying that I must fight in this war not with hatred or malice, but merely for defeating the forces of *adharma,* enabling *Dharma* to gain ascendancy thereby? That while the body may be engaged in fighting, the Heart must see it all as a part of a Divine Play already ordained by the Lord?

KRISHNA: By and large you seem to have got it right, which is encouraging!

You see Arjuna, there are three things–action, the thought behind the action and the feeling that inspires the thought. Action perforce has to be in the world where one necessarily has to deal with diversity. As for the thought, it does **NOT** have to be rooted in diversity.

ARJUNA: Why is that?

KRISHNA: Because, seeing diversity would merely enhance and aggravate whatever latent tendencies there might be for anger, jealousy, hatred, etc.

ARJUNA: Oh I see. So if a person attacks me in anger and I respond with anger, it would soon grow into a diverging spiral, is that it?

KRISHNA: That is exactly right. Anger always breeds more anger, hatred always breeds more hatred, and violence always begets more violence. People think they can quench violence with more violence; they might succeed temporarily, but in the long run, there would always be a counter reaction.

ARJUNA: Krishna, is this where *Prema* or Pure Love comes into the picture?

KRISHNA: Wonderful! You have got the point!

You see Arjuna, *Prema* is Divine. When the Mind, driven by the Heart, develops selfless and loving thoughts, actions can **NEVER** have a touch of anger, jealousy, or hatred.

In short, action **MUST** be in the world, appropriate to the circumstances leading to the action, but the **MOTIVATION** for the action must be based on **ETERNAL** considerations– that is what *Atma Dharma* is really all about.

ARJUNA: Is that how the Heart balances worldly action?

KRISHNA: Exactly.

ARJUNA: Lord, why don't we think and act like that? We say we love You and yet, there seems to be some problem with our Love; what exactly is that problem?

KRISHNA: I am glad you have asked that question.

Arjuna, you say you love Me. True; however, on close examination, your love would be found to be contaminated with selfishness! My Love never is, and that is the fundamental difference.

ARJUNA: Does that mean that Divine Love exists only in You?

KRISHNA: Not really. When humans are born, God sends them into the world with a full quota of Divine Love. However, by being careless, humans allow that gift of God to get contaminated; that is the real problem!

ARJUNA: And the Mind is the culprit that causes this contamination?

KRISHNA: Absolutely! The Mind is dragged by the senses into the external world, and if humans do not train to see God everywhere in the external world, they would soon forget God. Selfishness, greed, jealousy, etc., then have a golden opportunity to pollute the Mind, and that is how Divine Love, initially present in humans, starts getting contaminated.

Divine Love is present in every Heart. But when it flows out into the world through the Mind, the senses and the body, it almost invariably gets adulterated. It is this adulterated stuff that appears as attachment between mother and son, as infatuation between husband and wife, as desire between man and worldly attractions, and so on.

ARJUNA: Lord, I agree that Love in man can get polluted but surely the love man has for God is free from pollution.

KRISHNA: Arjuna, how I wish what you say is true! I have many types of devotees and in a manner of speaking, they all do love Me. However, almost everyone comes to Me with his or her own agenda!

ARJUNA: Really?! I never knew that!

There is a very important message in this Chapter which is, how we must be very much anchored in this world but react to it in a Divine way. From a historical point of view, this lesson was taught to humanity earlier when the Lord came as Rama. At that time, as a part of the Divine Drama, Prince Rama, then an adolescent, falls into depression. Sage Vasishta then counsels Rama, "teaching" Him what is called *Yoga Vasishtam,* wherein the same lesson was imparted. Bhagavan Baba refers to this as having our hands in Society but holding our heads aloft in the forest. What He means is that while our actions may be worldly, the motivations for those actions must be pure, as was the case with *Rishis* of yore.

Chapter 20

# CONCERNING *JNANA* AND *AJNANA* [KNOWLEDGE & IGNORANCE]

**Earlier, Krishna told Arjuna that He was imparting *Atma Jnana* or Knowledge of the Self; that was just a rough description of what He was doing. Krishna now explains that there is actually no need to impart *Atma Jnana* to anyone, since it is already latent within, having been put there by God in thoughtful anticipation. What then is the role of *Gurus,* who are normally supposed to impart Knowledge? That is the question answered in this Chapter.**

ARJUNA: Krishna, it is amazing that even to You, devotees come mostly with an axe to grind!

KRISHNA: What is so strange about it? Humans are always looking for a deal or a *quid pro quo;* it is as simple as that! They come to Me, offer prayers and in return, they ask for something–that is all.

ARJUNA: I am stunned; what more can I say? By the way, how many categories of devotees are there?

KRISHNA: Broadly speaking, one can identify four categories. All devotees love Me no doubt but, except for the devotees in category four, those in the other three want something or the other from Me.

ARJUNA: Lord, is it any surprise if devotees want something from You? Are You not our Eternal Father and Mother? From whom else could one ask for the things one wants?

KRISHNA: It is interesting Arjuna, you describe Me as the Eternal Father and Mother. Indeed that is true. But then, what most people want from Me has nothing to do with Eternity and that is the real pity!

ARJUNA: Is that so? What then do these devotees want from You?

KRISHNA: Oh, the usual sort of things.

ARJUNA: Such as?

KRISHNA: Well, devotees in category one want wealth, while those in category two want their problems solved and fixed.

ARJUNA: Frankly Krishna, You cannot blame them for that; after all, is not God the last refuge? What about devotees belonging to category three?

KRISHNA: Those I appreciate because they hunger for Spiritual Knowledge.

ARJUNA: What about the fourth category of devotees?

KRISHNA: They are the best, and they are called *Jnanis.* They want nothing, not even from Me. They just meditate on Me and experience Bliss.

Actually, I have no complaints about all this. No

matter to which category people belong, I love them all, and equally too. All are the same to Me, and I give to each what he wants.

ARJUNA: Krishna, I can understand Your appreciating the seekers and *Jnanis.* But what about the others who want something material? Why do You humour them?

KRISHNA: There are two reasons for that. Firstly, as I told you earlier, they too are My children, and so I oblige them also. Besides, there is a second reason.

ARJUNA: And that is?

KRISHNA: I give these people what they want because I hope that one day they would ask for what I would really like to give. Do you want to know what that is? Why, this very Knowledge of the Self or *Atma Jnana* that I am imparting to you right now!

ARJUNA: Lord, You are indeed the most compassionate One!

KRISHNA: Arjuna, it is funny people ask Me for all kinds of trivial things and trinkets, when I can confer the greatest possible boon.

ARJUNA: Lord, please can You clear yet another doubt?

KRISHNA: What is that?

ARJUNA: If I understand You correctly, man having come from God is intrinsically Pure, and it is during his stay on earth that he acquires impurities.

KRISHNA: That is right. When water comes down as rain it is pure, but if that water flows into a gutter, obviously rainwater would get polluted.

ARJUNA: How can man get rid of pollution?

KRISHNA: That is simple; by seeking a *Guru* and learning from the *Guru*.

ARJUNA: What does the *Guru* do?

KRISHNA: That is a good question. People normally think that a *Guru* imparts *Jnana*. This is pure nonsense! *Jnana* is God and since God is in you already, where is the question of the *Guru* giving you *Jnana?*

ARJUNA: I am bit confused Lord. If the *Guru* does not impart *Jnana,* then what exactly does he do?

KRISHNA: Well, the *Guru* does the obvious thing.

Let Me put it this way: Suppose a child goes out to play and comes back home rather dirty. What does the mother do?

ARJUNA: That is easy! The mother would clean the child.

KRISHNA: That is precisely what the *Guru* also does!

ARJUNA: I don't understand.

KRISHNA: What it means is that the *Guru* helps the student to get rid of all false notions, the cloud of ignorance. In short, the *Guru* does **NOT** impart *Jnana* but merely **REMOVES** *ajnana* or Spiritual ignorance in humans. When ignorance is removed, the *Jnana,* that is latent within, automatically shines.

ARJUNA: Lord, can You give an example so that I can understand better?

KRISHNA: Sure. Arjuna, sometimes the Sun is covered by the clouds; when the Sun is so covered, the level of ambient light goes down. When the cloud is blown away by the wind, the Sun becomes visible again and there is brightness all round. *Ajnana* or Spiritual ignorance is like a cloud that covers *Jnana* or the Divine Wisdom within.

ARJUNA: So the *Guru* is like the wind that blows away the cloud of ignorance?

KRISHNA: Exactly.

ARJUNA: And is that what You also do when You incarnate?

KRISHNA: Yes, to a large extent. Just recall what I was telling you earlier. I was talking mostly about the mistakes you were making, and those mistakes are the result of Spiritual ignorance.

ARJUNA: So Lord, You also are a *Guru?*

KRISHNA: You may say that; actually, the world refers to God as *Sadguru* or the *Guru* of *Gurus.*

ARJUNA: Lord, I simply do not know what to say! Here, in this world, we express gratitude to *Gurus* by offering *dakshina.* Lord, what *dakshina* should I offer to You?

**Since God is the Ultimate *Guru,* how fortunate are those who are born as contemporaries of the *Avatar!* However, this opportunity comes but rarely in human history. Having discovered that the Lord Himself has been acting as his *Guru,* Arjuna now wants to know what he must offer to the *Guru* of *Gurus;* the answer to that comes in the next Chapter.**

Chapter 21

# ALL ABOUT *BHAKTI* AND HOW TO BECOME DEAR TO GOD

**The conversation now veers round to the topic of *Bhakti*. In the *Gita* proper, Krishna teaches the famous *Bhakti Yoga* in the Twelfth Chapter, which is justly very popular. The essence of that is what Krishna now explains to Arjuna.**

KRISHNA: So you want to know what man must offer to God or the *Guru* of *Gurus?* Let Me tell you. Actually, I am very easy to please. Why, you could offer Me just a leaf, a flower or fruit and even water. Not difficult, is it?

ARJUNA: O Merciful Lord! What can I say, other than that You are most compassionate!

KRISHNA: Arjuna, do you know what it is that I would really like you and indeed all humans to offer to Me?

ARJUNA: What is that? Can there be anything simpler than water?

KRISHNA: Arjuna, you are not reading Me correctly. I do NOT want anything material. After all, leaf, flower, water and so on are all things that I have created; they really belong to Me. So what is the point in giving to Me something that I already have?

ARJUNA: Since, as You say, everything already belongs to You, what is it that we could offer? Frankly, I cannot think of anything!

KRISHNA: How about something non-material?

ARJUNA: Krishna, I am so overwhelmed that my Mind is entirely at a standstill! Please help me out by giving the answer Yourself!

KRISHNA: Very good; I shall oblige you. You see Arjuna, worldly *Gurus* have to survive, and so they accept, although somewhat reluctantly, money and material gifts. As for Me, I have everything; so, I suggest that you offer Me your bad habits.

ARJUNA: Lord, You cannot be serious! How can I offer bad habits to You?

KRISHNA: Why not? Arjuna, My suggestion is not so outrageous as you seem to imagine. Remember the famous story of the *Devas* and *Asuras* churning the Ocean of Milk? And what was the first thing to come out? Poison! And who swallowed it? The Lord! God is ready to accept your contamination so that **you may become Pure!**

ARJUNA: Lord, I am simply stunned! I now understand why devotees hail You as the Most Compassionate One!

KRISHNA: Time is running out Arjuna; you had better hurry up with your remaining doubts!

ARJUNA: I shall, dear Lord. You say You are Formless, but can also assume any Form, especially to please Your devotees. This being the case, I want to know how exactly am I to worship You? Should I worship You as the Formless God or as the God with Form? Of the two methods, which is better for me?

KRISHNA: Arjuna, I am glad you have asked Me this question for it is an important one.

Truly speaking, one can worship the Supreme One either as the Formless God or as God with Form.

ARJUNA: Yes, but which is better?

KRISHNA: Done sincerely, both types of worship would lead to the same goal, that is, merger with Me. However, considering the practical aspects, I would suggest that you focus on worship of God with Form. Indeed, this is the advice that I would give to 99.99 % of the devotees.

ARJUNA: Any particular reason why You say so?

KRISHNA: Sure. You see Arjuna, it is easy to say that God is without Form and all that, and that therefore He should be worshipped in the Formless aspect. He certainly can be, but that kind of worship is not easy I assure you.

ARJUNA: What's the problem?

KRISHNA: The problem is the Mind. Arjuna, man's True Nature is infinite and so is his Mind. But when man's outlook is largely external, being focussed on the world and the glittery things it offers, his vision becomes narrow. Tell Me, how can a person with limited vision, really and truly worship the Infinite?

ARJUNA: Krishna, does that mean that there is no hope for one who is immersed in worldly affairs? If that is true, what happens to people like me? I am a Kshatriya, and all my duties are in this world. How can I spend hours and hours meditating and all that?

KRISHNA: Arjuna, that **PRECISELY** is the issue I am addressing. I am well aware that simple folk who lead an ordinary life as a farmer, a carpenter, as a weaver, etc., cannot easily look inside and discover God within. So, what is the alternative? Simple: worship God with Form.

ARJUNA: Krishna, it is not so simple!

KRISHNA: Why do you say it is not simple?

ARJUNA: Because God can and does have so many forms! You are Narayana, Rama, Siva and so on! How am I to make a choice?

KRISHNA: [Laughs] Oh that! I understand your difficulty. Actually, there is no problem as you imagine.

ARJUNA: No problem at all? How come?

KRISHNA: Because you can worship God in any Form that pleases you!

ARJUNA: And You would not be bothered or annoyed?

KRISHNA: What a foolish thing to say! All Forms are Mine and Mine only! How at all can I be offended?!

Incidentally, one reason why God incarnates as a human and spends a long time here on earth is precisely to help man connect God with a definite Form.

ARJUNA: Sorry, can You please explain that again slowly?

KRISHNA: Sure. You see, when God incarnates with a human form, it gives mankind a good chance to see God, be in His company, talk to Him, directly experience His infinite Love and compassion, witness His miracles, serve Him physically, etc. In turn, this leads to stories about the *Avatar,* songs composed in His honour, and so on, all of which make worship of the *Avatar* so very easy, and build up a Heart to Heart relationship with Him. Every one of these activities promotes the worship of God with Form. Do you understand?

ARJUNA: So the simple thing would be to worship one's favourite *Avatar,* is that it?

KRISHNA: That's right.

ARJUNA: Krishna, people use idols to worship You. Is that right or wrong?

KRISHNA: Arjuna, that is a good question. People sometimes criticise idol worship; this is wrong. What is a mere idol for the critic is a live representation of the personal God for the devotee who is absorbed in worship. If a man has stone in his Heart, he will see merely a stone statue. But if a man has God in his Heart, the same stone would verily appear to him as God.

In short, it is all a matter of attitude. With the right attitude, even a picture would become God. But with the wrong attitude, even if God were to stand in front, the Divine aspect would be totally missed.

Thus, pictures and idols are **not** to be sneered at. They have their own place in the scheme of things, especially as the Form can help in leading to the Formless.

ARJUNA: In what way?

KRISHNA: Here is an example. I am now pointing with My forefinger at that hill, far away on the horizon. You first look at My finger, follow the direction in which the finger is pointing, and then look at the hill. Once you have seen the hill, the finger ceases to be relevant. It is the same thing with idols and pictures–they all point in the direction in which you must look. They lead you from the Form to the Formless–that is their utility.

ARJUNA: So, if I understand You correctly, idol worship is merely a stage, a starting point really, in the long road leading from God with Form to God without Form, am I right?

KRISHNA: Absolutely correct. Form is helpful but it always tends to restrict; one must therefore, at some stage, break out and see God everywhere, that is, experience the Omnipresence of God.

ARJUNA: Krishna, what must one do in order to become an ideal devotee of God? What are Your specifications for the ideal devotee?

KRISHNA: According to Me, an ideal devotee would treat pleasure and pain alike. He would neither go in search of trivial pleasures nor would he try to duck misery when it visits him. He never broods over the past nor worries about the future. Immersed in the present, he would be busy thinking of Me. For him, the present is no ordinary present–it is OMNIPRESENT!

ARJUNA: In what ways is the present so special?

KRISHNA: Well, the present did not come from nowhere; the past is the seed from which the present has emerged. And in the same way, the present is the seed for the future. Thus, the present links the past to the future.

ARJUNA: I can understand that as the flow of the timeline, but is there anything more to it?

KRISHNA: Of course; whatever is happening to you right now is the result of your past actions. It might be good or it might not be so pleasant. If suffering is what you are undergoing right now, there is no point in simply wasting time by wailing over the past; the past is past; it is over and gone.

ARJUNA: So what must one do?

KRISHNA: Is that not obvious? Instead of wasting time and crying about your past, just focus on getting everything you do now right, that is to say, you must ensure that all your present actions are perfectly Dharmic. That would automatically take care of your future.

ARJUNA: [slowly] I see. Anything more?

KRISHNA: Sure. My ideal devotee would have no trace of hatred in his Heart–not even an iota. Do you know why? Because hatred is sheer poison. I am Pure Love, Love that is nectarine. Can we have poison contaminating nectar? Never! That is why I say that a person who is free from hatred is dear to Me; got it?

ARJUNA: I think I do. What more?

KRISHNA: Ever balanced, the ideal devotee would never feel heady when praised nor depressed when criticised.

ARJUNA: Krishna, that is not easy!

KRISHNA: Sure it is not easy, but can you say that with practice you cannot do it? How can you say it is not possible, without even trying?

Arjuna, equanimity is what I like most, and equanimity means being balanced with respect to the opposites. One must be balanced in relation to everything that happens in one's life. If you possess equanimity, you can face life squarely and do not have to hide yourself in the forest. According to Me, equanimity is the best form of *Yoga*.

ARJUNA: Krishna, can everyone achieve equanimity or does one have to be a *Yogi* to achieve that?

KRISHNA: No Arjuna, you do **NOT** have to be a *Yogi*. Everyone can do it but one must try earnestly of course. It does not matter whether you are a soldier, a musician, or a cobbler. All that is required is to remain calm and accept things as they come. No matter what happens, such a person would always say, "This is good for me!"

ARJUNA: Krishna, what is the simplest way of achieving equanimity?

KRISHNA: Very simple! Just love all and serve all.

ARJUNA: That would help?

KRISHNA: Sure!

ARJUNA: How?

KRISHNA: Well, when you go out to help, say after an earthquake or some disaster like that, you would see a lot of people suffering. And when you see such suffering, you would realise the many blessings God has conferred on you. Thereafter, you would stop complaining about your problems and difficulties; that is how equanimity starts building up.

**The teaching Love All, Serve All, is the quintessence of Bhagavan Baba's Message, and is a beautiful summary of the entire *Gita,* and very practical too. This teaching is above all religions, going to the very core of human nature. Followed sincerely, it would not only promote equanimity, but also help one to see God in all persons, and therefore in Society as a whole. Thus it is that sometimes, Baba offers this teaching in the alternate words: Service to man is service to God.**

Chapter 22

# EPHEMERAL PLEASURE AND ETERNAL HAPPINESS

**Slowly, the dialogue is coming to an end, even as Arjuna clears a few residual doubts as a part of the winding up process. Presently, the discussion centres largely around how humans mostly tend to act keeping the short-term in view, whereas God expects them to be guided mainly by the long-term.**

KRISHNA: Arjuna, have we discussed enough, or are there still some points that you do not quite understand?

ARJUNA: Krishna, I am grateful to You for asking me, because there still are a few doubts I need to get clarified; after that I am through!

KRISHNA: Very well then, ask your doubts and better be quick about it.

ARJUNA: Krishna, I want to go back to this *Karma Phala Tyagam* business. I understand all that You said, but don't You agree that ambition is a great driving force?

KRISHNA: Did I ever tell you that I disagree? I am simply asking you why can't you let Love for God act as the motivating force rather than mere worldly ambition?

ARJUNA: Can God too be a motivator?

KRISHNA: Your question highlights the difference between the way ordinary humans think and the way God wants them to think.

ARJUNA: What do You mean by that?

KRISHNA: Arjuna, in life there are always two points of view, the short-term and the long-term. Humans calculate in terms of short-term return on investments and from that perspective, worldly ambition is certainly a very desirable quality. If short-term gain is the objective, then I have no argument.

ARJUNA: But You **did** raise an objection!

KRISHNA: That is because My perspective is long-term benefits for humans.

ARJUNA: Can You explain that?

KRISHNA: Sure. Arjuna, what I mean is the following: Driven by worldly ambition, a person makes a tremendous effort and might even succeed in attaining his goal. Fine. But does all that take you one inch closer to God? I doubt it!

ARJUNA: Krishna, what exactly are You getting at?

KRISHNA: Arjuna, worldly ambition is related to desire, and desire, I explained to you, binds you to this world, life after life. One entire birth is spent in short-term investment; then another birth is spent the same way; and so on it goes. What happens at the end of it all? Are you able to take even a small copper coin with you at the end of life? And when you are born again, you start doing the same old things once more! What for? Do you think that this time you can be smarter and take a huge bundle of gold or silver with you, when all others have failed? No way!

After chasing ambition life after life, have you moved closer to God? No! Does that not mean that you are essentially wasting the lives given by God to you repeatedly?

ARJUNA: You know Krishna, I never thought of it that way! To use the business language, we seem to make sure that God never gets any return on His investments!

KRISHNA: And yet, God keeps on backing humans, again and again. Isn't that amazing!

ARJUNA: Indeed it is! Tell me Krishna, why on earth does God keep on investing on man, over and over again?

KRISHNA: You fool, God is not like what you think; He does not make investments. Rather, He blesses you with an incomparable opportunity to get back to Him. And fools that humans are, they blow the golden opportunity every time!

ARJUNA: So, what must we do?

KRISHNA: What must you do? Change your perspective.

ARJUNA: From what to what?

KRISHNA: From the transient to the Eternal; from body-consciousness or *dehabbhimaanam* to God-consciousness or *Atmaabbhimaanam.* To use your language, from short-term perspective to the long-term perspective.

ARJUNA: And what happens after that?

KRISHNA: There you go, looking for returns again!

My dear Arjuna, did I not tell you that your True Nature is the *Atma,* that Bliss is the Nature of the *Atma,* that when you become united permanently with God, you would be in Bliss for ever?

Your ambition, what does it get you? Temporary happiness at best; when you succeed you are happy, but when you fail, are you still happy? With God, you would always be happy!

ARJUNA: Krishna, I am terribly sorry that I irritated You somewhat! I hope my next question would not elicit the same reaction!

KRISHNA: Well, what is your next question?

ARJUNA: You see Krishna, whether we like it or not, Creation is full of diversity; when we look around, we cannot help seeing diversity. And when we see diversity, we tend to respond to it also. This Atmic feeling or *Atmaabhimaanam* as You call it, is not easy!

KRISHNA: You have a point there. Arjuna, do you recall My telling you earlier that every human being is a composite of the gross body, the Subtle Mind and the Causal *Atma?*

ARJUNA: I do.

KRISHNA: Very good. Now bodies of different people are different; that is the way it is and one cannot do anything about it. Thus, at the level of the body, diversity is an inescapable empirical fact; you agree?

ARJUNA: Totally.

KRISHNA: Good to hear that. Let Me now go to the other extreme, namely to the level of the *Atma.* What kind of diversity do you think there is at that level?

ARJUNA: Krishna, I think You are trying to trap me with a tricky question!

KRISHNA: I am not doing anything of that sort; My question is very simple and you should easily be able to give me a straight answer.

ARJUNA: With that encouragement, I cannot disappoint You! Well, let me see; did You not tell me that there is only one *Atma?* So I guess that even though bodies are different, *Atma* is the same!

KRISHNA: Excellent! Arjuna, now think carefully. At the level of the bodies, there is a diversity; we cannot avoid that. At the level of the *Atma,* there simply cannot be any diversity. And yet, here we are, you and I, talking about diversity and all that. Why at all do you think this discussion has come up? Can you guess?

ARJUNA: Is it because of the Mind?

KRISHNA: Exactly. You see Arjuna, Creation has two faces; one face is that of diversity while the other face is that of Unity! What you see is what you want to see!

ARJUNA: What do You mean by that?

KRISHNA: Very simple. If the Mind is focussed on the world, it would tend to see nothing but diversity. However, if the Mind is focussed on the *Atma,* it would see nothing but Unity.

ARJUNA: [slowly] Oh I see; so the options are: either see diversity as Unity or Unity as diversity, is that it?

KRISHNA: Absolutely! It is not empirical diversity that is important, but the way one responds to it.

ARJUNA: I am not able to follow.

KRISHNA: Well, if one has the Atmic feeling, one would

never hurt anybody, no matter what the provocation.

ARJUNA: Now wait a minute! In this war that You are asking me to participate in, I would be injuring so many; is that not hurting?

KRISHNA: Arjuna, don't you know that the tongue and the Mind hurt much more than the knife and the sword?

The quality of the action is determined by the **intention** behind the action, rather than any discomfort caused by the action itself. A thorn enters a person's foot; his friend rushes to help and removes the thorn using another sharp thorn; some pain is caused no doubt, but does the person who is getting attention, accuse the benefactor?

ARJUNA: So Krishna, if I get You right, a person with body-consciousness or *dehabhimaanam* would see diversity even though everything in the Universe is tied together by Cosmic Unity, while a person with *Atmaabhimaanam* or *Atma Bhavam* would see Divine Unity even though others tend to see diversity–have I got it right?

KRISHNA: At last, you are there!

ARJUNA: That is great to hear!

The issue of short-term versus the long-term is far from trivial, especially in today's context. In the *Gita* proper, this issue is discussed in terms of *Preyus* and *Sreyus.* The former is all about worldly benefits and pleasures thereof, while the latter is all about uniting with God and enjoying permanent Bliss thereby. These days, the focus of people has become so limited that they do not even seem to be seriously concerned about the problems future generations would face as a result of our excessive consumption on the one hand, and mindless and almost uninhibited pollution of air, water and land on the other. How different it was with our ancestors who took care of all these treasures of Nature as trustees, and passed them on from generation to generation!

Chapter 23

# TOTAL SURRENDER IS THE BEST OPTION

**The curtain is about to come down on the immortal conversation between Krishna and Arjuna that fateful morning five thousand and odd years ago, in the battlefield in Kurukshetra. Arjuna has the last few doubts cleared up, and as per the Lord's command agrees to fight, in accordance with his *Atma Dharma*. For His part, Krishna uses the opportunity to give yet another remarkable assurance to mankind concerning the extent to which He would go, to take care of the one who surrenders to Him.**

KRISHNA: Hurry up Arjuna, what else do you want to know?

ARJUNA: Please bear with me, Krishna! There are just a couple of points left.

KRISHNA: Such as?

ARJUNA: Earlier, You talked about duty. Is anyone exempt from duty?

KRISHNA: None at all!

ARJUNA: Not even kings?

KRISHNA: No! Everyone from the monarch to the pauper **HAS** to perform his or her duty–no escape from that!

ARJUNA: What about Realised Souls? Surely, there is no need for them to perform any duty since they are already one with You.

KRISHNA: Actually, as long as they have a physical body, even saints and sages have a duty.

ARJUNA: What duty is that?

KRISHNA: That of guiding ordinary mortals on the Spiritual path.

ARJUNA: What about You?

KRISHNA: That is a good question! Technically, I have no duties to perform for I am **NOT** of this transient world, even though for purposes of incarnation, I have temporarily donned a human form. However, since people mostly see only My external human form, by way of setting an example, I too perform actions that could be called duty.

ARJUNA: Amazing! That shows how compassionate You are, dear Lord!

KRISHNA: Hurry up! What else?

ARJUNA: If You kindly permit, I want to go back to the topic of *Atma Dharma.* Please forgive me but don't You think that *Atma Dharma* and all that is a bit too much for ordinary folk, like say a farmer, a washerman, a carpenter, and so on?

I have studied with a *Guru,* learnt something of

the *Vedas* and all that. Yet, if You don't mind, I found what You just taught me to be rather heavy stuff!

Krishna, to put it very simply, have You got any easy formula for ordinary mortals? I mean something that they can easily adopt and use in day-to-day life, and still become one with You?

KRISHNA: [smiles] Arjuna, that is not only a good question but unknown to you, you have actually done a great service to millions, now and forever!

ARJUNA: Me? I have done that? How wonderful! I am dying to hear Your answer!

KRISHNA: Here it is, and make a good note of it.

First, always think of Me, and I really mean always. This becomes easy when you get into the habit of constantly chanting My Name.

Next, no matter what work you are doing or what action you are performing–and it must be good action by the way, and not an immoral one–think that you are **actually** doing it for Me, no matter who your worldly master might be. Remember, in the ultimate analysis, God is your Master. Perhaps you have forgotten, but this is actually a part of Vedic tradition; before any ritual is performed, the one who undertakes the ritual goes through a routine called *Sankalpa.* During that process, the person chants *Mantras* to indicate that whatever he is doing is for the pleasure of God–you must have heard the phrase *Bhagavat Preethyartham,* have you not? That is what I mean. Thus, what I am telling you is a mere reminder of what is already ordained in the scriptures.

ARJUNA: Anything more?

KRISHNA: Yes, and I am coming to that. The third and the final step is to just offer the action that is being performed to Me, that is all. What could be simpler?

ARJUNA: Two questions arising out of the above. Firstly, how exactly do I offer my actions to God? That is not clear.

KRISHNA: Offering to Me is extremely simple; it calls for just one word.

ARJUNA: What is that?

KRISHNA: *Krishnaarpanam!* I am sure you understand what it means; it means, "I offer this to You, O Krishna!" By the way, you must make this offering with Love, and **NOT** in a routine, bureaucratic manner!

ARJUNA: Let me see if I have got it right. First I must chant

Your Name always. Next, in my Heart I must continuously have the feeling that whatever it is that I am doing, I am doing it **entirely** for Your pleasure. And finally, I must cap it all by offering everything to You. Right?

KRISHNA: Wonderful!

ARJUNA: Now that I have learnt how exactly I am to make my offering to You, let me ask the remaining part of my doubt or my second question, which is: "What happens if one does all this?"

KRISHNA: True colours of a human! Always want to know, "What's there in it for me?"

Arjuna, if a person keeps on doing all the three things I say, then in the end, when he or she sheds the mortal coil, that person would come to Me for sure, and merge into Me for eternity. This I guarantee. What more can you ask for?

ARJUNA: Dearest Lord, there cannot be any greater illustration of Your compassion. In my ignorance and naiveté, I asked You a question that I ought not to have. Please forgive me!

KRISHNA: Arjuna, if you thought that the concession I just made was the height of compassion, let me tell you something that surpasses even that!

ARJUNA: Really?

KRISHNA: Yes. You know something? You simply do not

have to bother about anything, any rituals, any chanting, any scriptures or whatever.

Just surrender totally to Me!

Place **FULL** faith in Me, no matter what, like a kitten submits itself entirely to its mother. By the way, when I say **full** faith, I mean **full, complete, total and unwavering** faith, 24/7; not intermittent faith, understand?

If anyone does that, then I shall not only take total care of that person, but even absolve that person of any sin that he or she might perchance commit, unknowingly!

ARJUNA: Lord! This is astounding! Please can You kindly repeat that?

KRISHNA: I certainly shall, though in slightly different words.

Taking **TOTAL** refuge in Me and surrendering **UNCONDITIONALLY** to Me, relinquish to Me all your actions that you perform during your life as a part of your normal duties. I shall not only take full care of you, but even absolve you of all sins. This I assure you.

ARJUNA: Lord, I have no words with which I can respond to that! Even the gods in heaven would fail, if they tried.

KRISHNA: Very well then, at least now are you willing to pick up your bow and get ready to fight?

ARJUNA: Indeed my Lord, Thy word **SHALL** be done. Thus far, my Mind was clouded by mountainous ignorance. By your Divine Grace and Supreme Compassion, that ignorance has now been dispelled, and I shall plunge into the fight with full fervour, firm in my belief that You are the Doer and I am a mere instrument, involved in Your Divine Mission of putting *Dharma* back on its exalted pedestal.

KRISHNA: Arjuna, I am very pleased to hear that. There is one more thing I must tell you, over and above all that I said earlier.

ARJUNA: What is that my Lord?

KRISHNA: If you think about it carefully, it was not that I asked you to fight but asked you to do your duty. In life, duty is most important, and **no one is exempt from duty.**

Sustenance of *Dharma* is all about doing one's duty properly. You are a soldier, and therefore I instructed you about your duty by mentioning fighting. If it were someone else, say a trader, I would perhaps have said many of the things I told you differently. However, the focus would again have been on duty and duty alone.

In life, everyone must always adhere to his or her duty, in the situation that Destiny places one in; and this duty must be performed for its own sake, entirely **for the pleasure of the Lord,** and **not** with an eye on worldly benefits.

This is the simplest way to sanctify life and elevate even mundane actions to exalted heights, by transferring attention from the transient and the ephemeral to the Eternal. This is the only way to resonate to your True Nature, which, as I told you right in the beginning, is Divine.

Arjuna, what I have taught you might seem like a personal tutorial. Given the circumstances, it certainly was. Yet, this is an Immortal Message, and in its own way, would live as long as there is life in this Universe. Indeed, so sacred is this Message that even those who absorb and spread it would get elevated and receive My Grace.

I think I have said all there is to say; let Me now take the chariot back to our formation so that you may join your fellow warriors.

Don't worry Arjuna, everything would work out fine. As long as I am by your side, be assured that victory is yours!

**That brings to an end this unusual presentation of the Essence of the *Gita* in the form of an informal conversation between man and God.**

# THE *GITA* AND BABA'S TEACHINGS –SOME PARTING REFLECTIONS

### Introduction

I do hope you liked what you read in the preceding Chapters, and did not mind my taking certain liberties with the Immortal *Gita* in order to convey its essence in a manner suited to this day and age. In this "Epilogue", I would like to place the foregoing in a modern context, so that you can appreciate my motivation for attempting this unusual presentation of the Message of the *Gita.*

It should be obvious that I have not made any attempt to faithfully follow the Chapter sequence as they appear in the original classic; and I make no apologies for that either. My attempt was **not** to reproduce the *Gita,* but to convey its essence as I have understood it by listening to innumerable Discourses delivered by Bhagavan Baba, and by a careful study of many of His writings. As Baba often says, the *Gita* is all about duty, sincerely performed in the circumstances in which Destiny places us, but with an alignment to the Eternal rather than the transient; that is to say, duty must be performed with *Atma Bhavam* [as Krishna explains to Arjuna], rather than with worldly considerations, as we often tend to do.

What is the merit, if any, in attempting such an unusual presentation? That is what I shall try and explain presently. As a preamble, allow me to place before you a bit of my personal background. Firstly, I would like to mention that my formative years overlapped with many events in the thirties and forties, including the beginning of World War II, the Quit India

Movement, the terrible Bengal Famine, the dropping of the atom bombs, India's Partition, the bloodbath that came after Partition, and finally the assassination of Gandhi, all of which made their own impact.

Next, I would like to refer to my career as a scientist, most of it in the Department of Atomic Energy, a career that fired up my enthusiasm for Science, thanks to the inspiration provided by Jawaharlal Nehru, the first Prime Minster of India, and of course also by that remarkable scientist Homi Bhabha, who founded India's atomic energy and space programs.

The third point I wish to refer to is the failure of Science and Technology to solve the problem of massive poverty in India. I was always affected by poverty, especially rural poverty [of which I saw a lot during the two years I spent in a small village near Madurai at the height of World War II–there was a massive evacuation of all major cities, and my father who was then serving in Karachi sent me, my mother and my sister deep down to the South, to live with our grandmother]. While he was alive, Nehru constantly talked about S & T, especially when he was in the company of scientists. Nehru firmly believed that it was Science and Technology alone that could solve the problem of poverty in India. In my youth I was starry-eyed, and thus easily swept by the "success" of the Soviet Union [which greatly influenced not only Nehru but also others like the noted scientist Meghnad Saha and Subhas Chandra Bose] in eliminating material inequity to a large extent. Thus, it was no surprise that I fervently hoped that one day S & T would wipe out poverty in India. However, as the years rolled by, I realised how mistaken and naïve I had been to entertain such a belief.

After I retired from service in 1992, I came to Prashanti Nilayam to serve in the University here, the Sri Sathya Sai University, which I have been doing ever since. What attracted me to this place was the Message of Selfless Love and Service that Bhagavan Baba disseminated via every single action of His, including His mega projects. When I first came I knew very little about His teachings, but in the years that followed, I became fascinated by the manner in which Baba explained complicated aspects of Vedantic Philosophy in such a simple manner that even I could understand. As I heard more and more, I began to see amazing parallels between *Vedanta* and the frontiers of Modern Physics that border on Metaphysics; I was now firmly hooked!

As the years went by, I began to realise that *Vedanta* was not just heady and mystical philosophy; rather, there was a practical side to it with great stress on compassion, an aspect that was not only wonderful but breathtaking. And this appreciation increased when I read the *Gita* for the first time. It was then that I realised what Bhagavan Baba was doing all the time was to explain the subtleties and the nuances of the *Gita* in a manner that transformed the *Gita* from a philosopher's delight to an amazing and priceless **Manual for Life.** I finally understood why Gandhi always insisted on relying on the *Gita,* even when he was involved in politics. And it also dawned on me that the *Gita* held the magical key to solving complex problems that the human Mind is so good at creating. To put it differently, a careful analysis reveals that–and I have spent a lot of time analysing this matter–a good many of today's problems can [as I shall explain shortly] be ultimately traced to the Poverty of Love. While Science and Technology might be of some help in dealing with these problems, in the ultimate analysis, since Poverty of Love is the root cause of problems of Society–and I strongly believe they indeed are–S & T can **never** solve problems such as mass poverty, as Nehru [and many others like him including me at that time] passionately believed.

## Consciousness and Modern Science

With that preamble, let me now proceed to place the Krishna-Arjuna dialogue in the context of the teachings of Bhagavan Baba. Discourses on Spiritual topics are quite common in this country, but the thing that amazed me when I first started hearing Baba, or Swami as devotees refer to Him, was the constant emphasis He gave to the fact that every human being is a Spark of the Divine. He would often tell His students, "Don't behave like animals; remember you are humans first, and so start behaving like humans. However, you must not stop there, for indeed you all are the children of Immortality, that is to say, you all are the Embodiments of the Divine and the Eternal *Atma.* Hence, having reached the level of the human, you must then do all you can to ascend to the level of the Divine."

At this juncture, I would like to make two small digressions. Firstly, with respect to acting as humans, it might come as a surprise to many today that about half a century ago when the Cold War was getting very fierce and both America and the erstwhile Soviet Union were competing with each other in stockpiling deadly nuclear weapons by the thousands, Bertrand Russell and Albert Einstein led [despite much hostility in America], a vigorous campaign for a total ban on nuclear weapons of all kinds. In their manifesto, they said in part,

> ***We appeal as human beings, to human beings. Remember your humanity, and forget the rest. If you can do so, the way lies open to a new paradise; if you cannot, there lies before you the risk of universal death.***

You would see from this profound appeal how important it is that we should never forget that **we are actually human beings and must, by the manner in which we act and behave, justify the form we are blessed with, namely the human form!** Incidentally, it is ironic, as Bhagavan Baba sometimes points out, that although humans appeared on earth about two hundred thousand years ago, the humanness latent in them, is yet to manifest in full bloom on a large enough scale.

My second point relates to the *Gita* where Krishna emphatically declares that **He is the Primordial Seed from which every single entity in the Universe has emerged.** I make a pointed reference to this because Modern Science asserts–and there is a lot of scientific evidence for making such an assertion–that the entire physical Universe and all that it contains, emerged from just one event, popularly referred to as the Big Bang. According to the best estimates now available, and they are fairly accurate, the Big Bang took place about 13.8 billion years ago. In other words, if *Vedanta* declares One became Many, Modern Science also says the same, with respect to inert matter of course.

This brings me to the issue of Consciousness. If there is one remarkable thing about a living being, it is that it is **aware** that it exists. As it stands, Science today is unable to explain where this self-awareness comes from. Many scientists take the view that Science might never be able to explain Consciousness. Others claim that while presently Science has not been able to come up with any explanation, there is really nothing very mysterious about Consciousness; it is all a product of evolution, higher-order brain activity, etc. The latter view is particularly popular with evolutionary biologists.

As a physicist, I sharply disagree with this category of biologists. If we go by the recent discoveries in particle physics, then any physical property an elementary particle is found to possess, **must have been latent** in something more fundamental. I hope I am not taxing you too much, but may be I could [with the bit of hand-waving that becomes inevitable when one descends to popular science!] say the following:

Consider the ubiquitous electron. These days even schoolchildren know that the electron is a tiny particle having negative electric charge. The question is, where did this charge come from? And the answer to that is that the electro-magnetic field, which is the primordial agency that controls all electro-magnetic phenomena, inherently has features that allow the electron to acquire a charge when it manifests as a particle. Maybe I have not really helped with your understanding but the point I am really trying to make is that something simply **cannot** come out of nowhere; it **must** have been latent in something else that is the "**parent**". In Physics, we have many types of fields, and the various elementary particles we know can all trace their "parentage" to one or the other of these fields. The important point is that the exotic properties that these basic building blocks of matter are known to possess, **have an inherent latency in the parent field.**

Leaning on this, I believe that the "unknown something" from which the so-called Big Bang originated, **also** had latent in it, Consciousness. Thus, if later in evolution Consciousness manifested in living beings [to a greater and greater extent as the species evolved], it was really a case of latency slowly revealing itself step by step. If, as we all believe, and indeed as Krishna declares, that everything came from God, then clearly, God must be Absolute Consciousness. It is interesting that *Vedanta* asserts precisely that via the declaration: *Prajnaanum Brahma,* which means Consciousness is God.

Further analysis shows that this Pure or Absolute Consciousness [which, incidentally is the same as *Niraakara Brahman* that Krishna refers to], manifests in the physical Universe in various ways. At the lowest level, it reveals itself as the capacity to be aware of the external world. At a somewhat higher level, it manifests as the Individual Conscience of humans, that acts as a Moral Compass. And when the individual realises that the so-called Indweller within him or her is the same as the God residing in every other Heart, the person concerned becomes awakened to the Universality of God and His Omnipresence.

Adding now to what Krishna has already told Arjuna, I might perhaps draw attention to some perspectives from Modern Physics that strongly corroborate the all-pervasive nature of Universal Consciousness. Unfortunately, I cannot go here into all the details, which start with the fascinating developments associated with the early years of quantum mechanics. That was when Einstein, who strongly believed in the causal aspect of Nature, expressed grave doubts about Niels Bohr's interpretation of the philosophical principles underlying quantum mechanics. Later, after many tense debates with Bohr, Einstein reluctantly conceded that quantum mechanics did work; however, he always felt that it was unsatisfactory and that a future theory would displace it totally. That, however, has not happened; instead, quantum mechanics has flowered enormously since then, becoming the mainstay of almost all developments of Modern Physics.

Along the line, a major development has been that in the seventies of the twentieth century, a series of landmark experiments meant to critically examine a certain objection of Einstein, surprisingly revealed that there was a strange, totally unexpected and mysterious global connectivity underlying the **entire Universe.** Commenting on it, scientist Gary Zukov says in his book ***Dancing Wu Li Masters,***

> ***The philosophical implication of quantum mechanics is that all things in our Universe [including us] that appear to exist independently are actually parts of one all-encompassing organic pattern and that no parts of that pattern are ever really separate from it, or from each other ...In short, the physical world, according to quantum mechanics is not a structure built out of independently existing unanalysable [indivisible] entities, but rather a web of relationships as a whole.***

Professor Geoffrey Chew of the University of California gives expression to the same idea by remarking,

> ***Your electrons and mine are only approximately distinguishable. In denying objective reality***

> ***[that Einstein vehemently stood by], quantum mechanics denies absolute status to your individuality. The only individual is the entire Universe.***

I would say that all these are huge hints that, underlying what our senses perceive as a Universe packed with diversity, there exists an **unseen substratum** that provides a global connectivity that indeed unifies everything–this, by the way, is the conclusion of Modern Physics! It is therefore not unreasonable to suppose that the *Atma* pervades the whole of Creation, although it is not visible, even as the thread that holds the pearls of a necklace is not seen. *Vedanta* succinctly describes this by stating that for the seen, the unseen is the basis. Similarly, while recording a Spiritual Message to the world during his trip to England in 1931 at the time of the Second Round Table Conference, Gandhi said, "There is an indefinable mysterious power that pervades everything; I feel it though I cannot see it."

I trust I have said enough to at least bring to your notice the fact that many concepts of *Vedanta* **do** seem to find corroboration in the findings of Modern Science. I would next like to turn the focus on Consciousness, but before I do that I must make a reference to some amazing and pioneering experiments performed by Professor Robert Jahn of Princeton University. Professor Jahn started his career as an aeronautical engineer, but along the line, almost by accident, he became involved in experiments on para-psychic phenomena. When he started, he was a complete sceptic and performed these experiments partly to convince himself that such phenomena did **NOT** exist, and were the result of pure imagination. But strangely, his experiments told him otherwise; however, he continued to disbelieve his results, suspecting there might have been errors and lack of sufficient controls. He laboured on for decades and eventually was forced to the conclusion that Consciousness **did** exist, and that it could actually influence inert matter! Jahn went even further to assert that Consciousness was like the many fields already known in Physics.

This was clearly a most revolutionary idea, and naturally, it did not find favour with a large number of establishment scientists. Sometimes, it takes many years to overcome prejudice, and where bias is concerned, even scientists could be quite unscientific! Even so, like Robert Jahn did, many leading Western scientists, each in their own way, have conceded and eventually accepted many of the principles of *Vedanta.* David Bohm was one of these, and commenting on the Vedantic view of Reality, he says,

> ***In this [the Vedantic] view, the entire structure and order of forms, proportions, and "ratios" that present themselves to ordinary perception and Reason are regarded as a sort of veil, covering the true reality which cannot be perceived by the senses, and of which nothing can be said or thought.***

I might add that Bohm spent many years trying to develop a scientific theory of what he called Implicate Order, to describe this Reality, to the extent it was accessible to Science.

Next, I would like mention the name of Professor George Wald of Harvard University, a Noble Prize winner, who also supports the view that the Universe is pervaded by Consciousness. He says,

> *It came to me quite lately, as a new and extraordinary idea, both tempting and repellent, since it shocked my scientific sensibilities. Then I realised with some embarrassment that many others had been there before–not only mystics over past millennia, but also a few most thoughtful physicists quite recently.*
>
> *It is the view that, just the contrary of Consciousness appearing as a late outgrowth of evolution of life on this and other planets, that this Universe breeds life and Consciousness, because Consciousness is its source, because the stuff of this Universe is ultimately mind-stuff. What we recognise as the material of the Universe, the Universe of space-time and elementary particles and energies is actually an Avatar, the materialisation of Primal Consciousness. In that case, there is no waiting for Consciousness to arise. It is always there, at the beginning and at the end. What we wait for in the evolution of life is only the culminating Avatar, the emergence of self-conscious bodies that can articulate Consciousness, that can give it a voice, a culture, literature and art, and science.*

This is indeed a most remarkable, though a somewhat reluctant admission, by a Western scientist of eminence! Erwin Schoredinger, one of the discoverers of quantum mechanics [for which he won the Noble Prize] also came to the conclusion that the *Atma* was the Ultimate Reality.

At this point, I perhaps need to assure you that I have neither lost my way nor am I rambling! All the foregoing was by way of stressing two major points:

1. Everything in the Universe, from the atom to the galaxies [and that includes us] has a hidden and subtle connectivity. That is what is referred to as the *Atma,* God, Pure or Absolute Consciousness, call it what you will. Interestingly, the existence of a subtle substratum is corroborated by Modern Science, though I must admit, it does not ascribe to it the attributes that *Vedanta* does [such as Love and Compassion, to which I shall come shortly].

2. The Universe has undergone an evolutionary process, with three strands associated with this evolution. The first strand deals with the evolution of **inert** matter, all the way from elementary particles to gross matter and even consolidated objects like stars and planets. The second strand deals with the evolution of life from the most primitive form of life believed to have appeared on earth about 3.5 billion years or so ago, to humans, whose appearance is very recent. The third strand relates to the blossoming of (latent) Conciousness in living beings, seen at its best in humans. Where the latter are concerned, some individuals are quite evolved in this respect, like for example, the sages and those whom we call realised souls; others [and clearly this applies to over 99 % of the human population!] are obviously not.

### The slow unravelling of Pure Consciousness in Creation

With this background on hand, I am now in a position to

place before you three quotes that are very pertinent to the above. They are:

***He who lives on earth must become man first,***
***Then, he has to learn the way to God,***
***And discover the delight of the Spirit.***
***This is the Raja Yoga that the Vedas teach.***

***Poem by Baba***

***I died a mineral and became a plant.***
***I died a plant and rose an animal.***
***I died an animal and I was man.***
***Why should I fear? When was I less by dying?***
***Yet once more shall I die, to soar***
***With blessed angels; but even from angelhood***
***I must pass on. All except God perishes.***
***When I have sacrificed my angel soul,***
***I shall become that which no mind ever conceived.***
***O, let me not exist! For Non-Existence proclaims,***
***"To Him we shall return."***

***Sufi poet Rumi***

***Just as minerals became the trees, the trees give rise to animate life, and lower animals evolved into man, so too should man evolve further and become God.***

***Bhagavan Baba***

I might add that someone [whose name escapes me], paraphrased all this as follows: "Consciousness sleeps in a stone, stirs in a plant, awakens in an animal, and flowers in a human." I hope you have noticed that the sequence of evolution indicated in all these various statements overlaps considerably with the observations of Professor George Wald that I presented earlier. Of course, Wald does not refer to the further evolution of human Consciousness to a stage where it becomes one with Universal Consciousness.

Bhagavan Baba gives a beautiful analogy to explain this last step. He says that a human being is like a balloon with air in it, the air being the analogue of the *Atma*, while the skin of the balloon is the counterpart of the body and the Mind. Swami says that as long as the balloon retains its inflated shape, the air inside is trapped; however, when the balloon bursts, the trapped air escapes, merging with the atmosphere surrounding the balloon. In the same way, as long as the body and the Mind hold sway functioning as the Ego, the *Atma* remains "trapped"; however, when attachments are sublimated, the "trapped" *Atma* becomes free, and one is "liberated". That is the last stage in the evolution of the individual "soul", namely the merger of the individual Consciousness with Universal Consciousness.

All this is an intellectual discourse on the human Spirit, its origin, its evolution and its ultimate destination. But does it have any practical implication, especially to today's world and the various problems that humanity faces? Indeed it does, and in my opinion, no one has explained this more clearly than Bhagavan Baba. It is to this aspect of the *Gita* and Baba's teachings that I shall now turn.

## The relationship between the individual, Society and Nature

Baba often says that there is a "limb-hierarchy" associated

with Creation that is as follows: First, there is the *Vyashti* or the individual. Next, every individual is a part of *Samashti* or Society; in that sense, the individual is a limb of Society. For its part, Society does not stand all by itself, being a part of Nature or Creation, for which the Sanskrit name is *Srishti.* Thus, Society or *Samashti* may be regarded as a limb of Nature or *Srishti.* And finally, Nature having been created by God, can be regarded as a limb of *Parameshti* or God Himself. We thus have a quartet–*Vyashti, Samashti, Srishti,* and finally *Parameshti,* each of the first three forming a limb of something larger than itself.

Baba then goes on to point out an interesting and very significant analogy between Society and a living human body. As all of us are aware, the cell is the basic building block of the human body; in this sense, the cell is analogous to the individual, even as the body as a whole is analogous to Society. Baba now says that if we study carefully how the human body functions as a self-organised system, we would get all the tips we need to make Society run smoothly. In other words, says Swami, all that humanity has to do is to emulate the "operating system" that a healthy human body follows. If we implement that, we would have a healthy Society!

Let us examine this a bit deeper. The various organs of the body are built up from cells; in the same way, groups of individuals make up communities or functional units like a school, a hospital, an office, a police station, etc. Next, just as we have various systems in the human body made up of a set of organs, like the digestive or the respiratory system, for example, so also in Society, we have various systems like the financial system, the administrative system, the health-care system, and so on. Finally, just as the different systems together constitute the total human body, so also in human affairs, the totality of all [man-made systems] constitute Society. Needless to say that for the body to remain healthy, the different systems must work in perfect harmony–this much is not difficult to follow.

Now comes an important issue. Is there any basic principle that all the constituent units of the human body from the cell upwards follow? Yes there is: ***All for one and one for all,*** [which of course is the motto of the Muskcteers of Alexander Dumas' famous novel]. To put it differently, in the human body there is **no** selfishness at any level; rather, every constituent unit works as a "Trustee" for common good. Trusteeship–that is the key word I was leading up to.

### Trusteeship, the only way out

Few are aware that the concept of Trusteeship applied to Society as a whole is strongly implied in the *Gita.* One of the few who understood it was Gandhi, and during his life, he strongly advocated it. The Trusteeship concept is always met with scepticism, although, in reality, humanity is already practicing it in limited areas. Further, there is currently a strong drift in that direction in many domains, although most people are unaware of it; more about all that shortly.

Collecting the main points made thus far, we have the following:

1. Underlying humanity and indeed Nature, there is **one** unifying thread that connects everything, and that is a Divine strand.

2. If we become strongly conscious of that underlying

unity, then we would see Unity in Diversity, instead of interpreting the Hidden Cosmic Unity in terms of a superficial diversity.

3. At the practical level, while the Heart must generate feelings of Unity, the body and the Mind must steer actions in such a way that is appropriate to the circumstances involved, echoing at the same time the overall Divine Unity that binds us all.

4. Taking a clue from the way the constituent units of a healthy human body function, Society must function in **total** harmony at **all levels,** from the macro to the nano.

5. Stated differently, since Society is a "living" entity made up of constituent units that are themselves living entities [namely humans], the ideal "Operating System" for Society would clearly have to be the same or at least a close parallel of what operates in a healthy human body.

A body become sick when a group of cells do not function the way they are supposed to. In the worst case, the cells go totally out of control, behaving in a completely random, arbitrary and independent manner; that is when the body becomes afflicted with cancer. In the same way, when individuals forsake *Sathya* and *Dharma,* Society can end up with all kinds of problems, ranging from being a "sick Society" to a "failed Society" in which complete anarchy prevails. That extreme anarchy could indeed become the fate of Society was wonderfully anticipated in ancient Indian scriptural texts, wherein there are frightening descriptions of what could happen in the Kali Age. Sadly, many of those terrible forecasts seem to be coming true; all of which strongly stress the need to return to the basics. Those basics are to be found in the *Gita,* while illustrations of the basics are provided by the lives of the *Avatars,* as well as of saints [of all countries].

Summarising all of the above, the Message of Krishna and of Baba reduce to the following:

- Since everyone has the Divine Spark within, all humans are indisputably the Embodiments of Pure Love.
- However, attracted by distractions that the world is full of, the senses and the Mind, create a cloud of ignorance [*ajnana*], as a result of which actions of individuals start deviating from *Sathya* and *Dharma.*
- The combined aberration of a large number of individuals then begins to impact Society at a macro level, which is when Society starts becoming "sick".
- Depending on the extent of deviations and aberrations, the nature and seriousness of the "sickness" could also vary.
- At the practical level, large inequities manifest in a sick Society as a sharp divide between the so-called "haves" and the "have-nots".
- While many are the reasons for inequities to appear, the root cause in most cases is the "Poverty of Love".

**How Poverty of Love leads to innumerable problems**

It is now necessary to examine how exactly Poverty of Love can and does lead to a host of problems. Sometime ago, the noted American Economist and thinker, Professor Jeffrey

Sachs of Columbia University, delivered several lectures over the BBC, as a part of the Reith Lecture Series. Prof. Sachs analysed in detail the problems currently facing humanity, how they arose, and might perhaps be solved. Prof. Sachs believes that technology holds the key, but in my view, we must look elsewhere for real and meaningful solutions.

According to Professor Sachs, the three basic problems humanity now faces are: 1) The threat of increased conflict and indeed large-scale war, 2) the threat of climate change, enhanced particularly by humanity's reckless consumption, leading in turn to extensive pollution, and 3) last but not the least, massive poverty. I cannot go into these issues in detail here, but if you think about it, all these three issues could ultimately be traced to what I refer to as the "Poverty of Love". Let us examine this a bit more closely.

Conflict always starts with anger, which, degenerating into hate, quickly leads to the tipping point. Anger usually arises when there is a contention for something material that two [or sometimes more than two] parties want. Conflict could also be the result of someone trying to take away the identity or the cultural space of another person or community. At the root of it all, two or more persons, or communities, or groups, or even countries, try to stress differences, and get overwhelmed by the feeling of what Swami refers to as the "mine" and "thine" feeling [*dehabhimaanam* or body-consciousness as Krishna explains to Arjuna]. Closely aligned to body-consciousness are greed, selfishness, jealousy etc,. all of which arise due to absence of Selfless Love. If, however, Selfless Love prevails, then there would be no "ownership" fights or conflicts; instead, the feeling of "share and care" would take over. If you think through the details, I am sure you would become convinced that conflicts **CAN** be resolved if trust and Selfless Love replace suspicion and hate; and it really does not cost all that much, except a firm will and deep determination.

Next, let us consider climate change. Everyone knows it is caused by carbon footprint. What is the simplest way to reduce this footprint? **Ceiling on desires!** Few appreciate the fact that right from the mid-eighties, economists have been warning that the rate at which non-renewable resources are being consumed by the advanced countries would not only ruin the planet in many ways, but, in addition, would leave very little of these resources for future generations. However, all that did not stop the rich from proliferating their wants, and go into a consumption spree as if there was no tomorrow. Then came disturbing signals in the form of unusual weather and climate patterns, followed by detailed scientific studies, all which clearly revealed that it was humans who were creating climate change.

Since then, there have been innumerable conferences and meetings to address the issue, invariably ending up with many pious declarations but little action. When it comes to brass tacks, the developed countries tell India and China, "You better do something about it, for your rate of growth is more than ours." India and China retort, "But listen, you have already reached an advanced state, and in absolute numbers, it is you who are consuming more! Besides, what about the huge pollution burden you have already created?" So on the argument goes, with both sides arguing that the other party is to blame. And where does all this finger-pointing leave millions and millions of ordinary people all over the world? The answer is clear, is it not? Self-interest and selfishness take root only when there is Poverty of Love, which means that the second major problem identified by Sachs **also** can be traced to the same root cause.

As for physical poverty, people say, "You know how much money it would cost to remove the massive poverty that prevails now? Where is the money?" I am not sure lack of money is the real cause. Just look at the amount of money spent on arms, unnecessary high-tech wars and conflicts, on gambling and such other "sin" industries that exist merely for providing sense gratification in various ways. Just look at the luxury industry and how much of money is wasted in that. If, as Krishna and Baba teach us, we learn to see God in all suffering humans, and if we **REALLY** love God, would we allow the suffering that prevails while a few wallow in shocking luxury?

Many with whom I have passionately discussed such issues say to me, "Listen, it is wonderful to quote Gandhi and say that there is enough to satisfy the needs of the whole of humanity but not enough to satisfy the greed of one person and so on. All this 'quotational wisdom' takes us nowhere, because you are missing one basic point. Greed is a basic nature of human beings."

I sharply disagree because that is **NOT** what Krishna has taught us. He says, "O man, you have come from **ME!** You are thus the Spark of the Divine!" Baba too asserts the same, reminding us again and again that we are the children of Immortality. If Divinity is our True Nature, then clearly greed has crept in as a contamination. Instead of wanting to scrub ourselves Spiritually clean, we try to take the easy route by pleading our inability to be Selfless. This is where our proclaimed Love for God is put to real test. If we **REALLY** love God, then we **HAVE** to do as per His bidding.

**Selfless Love is the only anti-dote to Poverty of Love**

It is not out of place at this juncture, to draw specific attention to some of Baba's Missions that illustrate very powerfully how Selfless Love can and does actually work in this day and age. However, before I get on to that, it might be useful to give a thumb nail sketch of Baba's life, especially for the benefit of those who are not aware of the biographical details. Baba was born in 1926 as Sathyanarayana Raju in a poor family in a small hamlet called Puttaparthi [in Anantapur District of what is now Andhra Pradesh] that did not even have a direct road leading to it. Though He did very well in studies, young Raju left home and school way back in October 1940, making service to humanity His prime objective. His family was stunned, naturally, since everyone was looking upon Him as the potential saviour; and why not, considering that He was brilliant in studies and excelled in school? Who could say that young Raju would not have become a great ICS officer in the British Government [the ultimate in good fortune in those days] ending the perpetual misery of the family? Imagine their shock, seeing all their fond hopes going up as smoke in a flash!

Satyanarayana Raju, who from that fateful day became known to the world as Sri Sathya Sai Baba, might have left every one shaking their heads but over the years, He has not only shown what Selfless Love really is, but also that it **actually** works. How else does one explain the fact that in 1981, He founded a University in what was once truly a "God-forsaken" village, when almost everyone said it cannot be? How else does one explain the even more staggering fact that on 23rd November 1990 [His 65th Birthday], Baba announced to a mammoth crowd that exactly one year from that day, a Super Speciality Hospital would start functioning in Puttaparthi in which cardiac surgery would be performed completely free, and that such a Hospital **did** come into existence exactly on the day forecast, and has been functioning ever since offering free, the best of Healthcare to the poor?

As for the University, the important thing is not that it was established in a village, not even the fact that it offers free education at a time when education has become a full-fledged business, but the incredible importance given to character development. Why is Baba doing all this? To send a powerful message, concerning which I shall say more presently.

As for the Super Speciality Hospital that Baba declared would start functioning in one year, let me state as an eye-witness, that on the morning of 22nd November 1991, the then Prime Minister of India, Mr. P. V. Narasimha Rao actually inaugurated the Hospital. Yes, the Super Speciality Hospital **HAD** come into being in **exactly** one year, and that too in a **village!** Even more amazing, four cardiac surgeries were performed on that inaugural day, all on poor patients from neighbouring villages, and absolutely free; and so it has been ever since.

Today that Hospital offers services in Cardiology, Urology, Orthopaedics, Ophthalmology, and Reconstructive Surgery, and tens of thousands of patients from all over India have been treated free, everyone without exception. When I say free, I mean everything from the first consultation, the subsequent diagnostics and detailed investigations [that include ECG, Doppler scans, X-ray and CT scans and even gamma scans], procedures that range from angiography to heart-valve replacements and insertion of pacemakers, the medicines, the stay in the wards, both ICU and general, and the food– everything is **ABSOLUTELY FREE**, no matter who the patient happens to be. Not a single penny is charged, nor is any donation sought from the patients treated. In fact, there is no cash counter in the Hospitals: indeed, there is no provision whatsoever for paying donations within the Hospital premises; even the word money is kept out of the view of patients. Baba is firm that there should be no solicitation of donations. In fact, anyone visiting the Hospitals would hear regularly on the PA system, announcements in various languages that no money should be paid to anyone under any circumstances.

By way of completion and for the record, I must state that a second Super Speciality Hospital was established in Bangalore in 2001, where treatment is offered in the areas of cardiology and neurology. Once again the best of treatment, with absolutely no payment whatsoever. The University and the Hospitals of Baba by no means exhaust His various socially-oriented Missions, but I shall skip references to them and instead deal with two questions: 1) How does Baba manage to run a [private as opposed to a Government funded] University without charging any fees whatsoever? 2) Likewise, how does He manage to run two Super Speciality Hospitals where heart and brain surgeries are performed every day in a routine manner and the best of treatment is offered without charging one paisa?

According to an old adage, where there is a will, there is a way. For Baba it is: "Where there is Pure Love and the burning urge to serve, anything is possible." It is of course quite difficult to believe this at the present time, when selfishness has become so rampant. That precisely is the reason why Baba has undertaken His various Missions; it is important therefore, to spend some time understanding the "chemistry" of Pure Love.

We must remember that Baba plunged into service at the young age of fourteen, living in a village that was quite backward, indeed even as late as the eighties. But that exactly was His point: To show that even great handicaps and seemingly impossible difficulties can be overcome by plugging into Pure Love which, as Krishna explained to Arjuna, God blesses all with. The early years were quite difficult, but Baba was ever determined; as He often says, if we want to succeed, we must have lots of Self-confidence. I must here clarify that as used by Swami, the word Self-confidence, **DOES NOT** imply an "I-can-do-it" type of egoistic belief; rather it means having full confidence in the Real Self or the *Atma* that is the core of one's being. In other words, one must work with the faith and belief that God with His infinite power, would make it all happen, provided one works Selflessly.

To get on with the narration, while engaged in His various Missions Baba faced difficulties galore, but all of them got solved. How? Well, as the years went by, more and more people heard of Bhagavan Baba and His passionate commitment to Selfless Service. When they came to see Him and have His *Darshan*, they were invariably bowled over, and in due course, hundreds of people pitched in silently and in various ways to make **everyone** of His Missions happen. It was the **momentum generated by an invisible fabric of Love** that bound one and all of His followers, making many amazing things to happen, otherwise hard to imagine.

Let me give just one example to make my point and I hope most emphatically; and by the way, these observations are made as a personal witness. On the 19th of January, 2002, Baba went to Bangalore to participate in the celebration of the first anniversary of the Super Speciality Hospital there. I was present in the audience when, as expected He delivered an address. Suddenly and in a most unexpected manner, in the midst of His Discourse, Baba announced that the people of Madras [now Chennai] were going through tremendous suffering on account of continued failure of the monsoon, and did not have water even for drinking since all the lakes that normally supplied the city had gone totally dry. Water was being brought in by tankers and even train.

Digressing for a moment, let me here state that water scarcity has been a chronic problem in Madras for as long as I can remember, and for years people were talking agitatedly about it; however, little happened. And then one fine day, the Governments of Tamil Nadu and Andhra Pradesh started collaborating to build a long canal that would bring the waters of the Krishna river to Madras–a longstanding dream. It took nearly a dozen years for the canal to be completed but when it was finished, it hardly solved the problem. Reason? Very poor construction. Result? After spending a lot of money, the people of Chennai were still in square one. Meanwhile, the suffering of the citizens of that great metro began to reach intolerable heights.

Getting back to Baba's Discourse I was referring to, He suddenly announced that He was going to bring relief to the citizens of Chennai. No one had made a specific appeal to Him, but having already executed a mammoth drinking water project in Anantapur District [of Andhra Pradesh] that brought relief to about a million people spread across about nine hundred villages, Baba decided, just like that, that He would come to the help of the citizens of Chennai also. Believe it or not, the entire canal meant to bring water from river Krishna was redone using the most modern technology; as a result, within two years, there was a **brand new** canal stretching over a hundred kilometres, built by the Sri Sathya Sai Central Trust. Since that time, the citizens of Chennai [with a population of about eight million] have not had any drinking water problems! It may all sound like a fairy tale, but the miracles of Pure Love are more staggering and mind boggling than any fairly tale can be.

Where exactly is the magic? That is what Baba is seeking to demonstrate all the time. Many think that given money, problems can be solved. Yes, money **IS** needed; but something more always went into all of Baba's projects, and that was the invisible texture of Love which performed its own magic. As Mr. A. Ramakrishna [then of Larsen and Toubro, the company that executed all of Baba's major projects, including the various drinking water projects] told me, in every project, there are glitches, disputes, and so on, to resolve which often takes a lot of time, leading to project delays. In the case of Baba's projects, Mr. Ramakrishna added, such delays hardly occurred. Once the public knew that Baba was sponsoring the project, everyone did all they could to help and facilitate the project in every possible way. Governments waived taxes, suppliers offered products [such as steel and cement] at a rock-bottom price, workers worked with great enthusiasm [which Baba frequently acknowledged by presenting them with clothes, watches and so on], Government officials co-operated, and even ordinary people helped in amazing ways. For example, during the Anantapur project, the huge water pipes often had to be laid and taken through private land to take shortcuts and reduce costs. Normally this is an almost impossible task, with landowners making excessive demands for payment. But in this case they just said, "Swami is giving us water and we must do all we can do help Him!"

That shows Pure Love works silently and in mysterious ways. In fact, I can go further and corroborate this from personal experiences of mine in the University, and what I have personally witnessed in the Super Speciality Hospitals, especially the one in Prashanti Nilayam. Where the University is concerned, people come forward in amazing ways to serve and help. The primary source of support is of course donations which come because people at large are not only captivated by Baba's Love, but also strongly believe in His Mission. Many donate in kind rather than with cash, the contributions ranging from small things such as musical instruments for the University brass band, books and journals for the library, computers, all the way to multi-media facilities and internet connection between the various campuses. At the time of the Annual Sports and Cultural Festival, people from the army come forward to train our students in all sorts of things from aero sports to dare-devil motor cycle stunts. Then there are professors from America and Canada who regularly come here to spend time teaching, as a token of Love for Baba and as a service. Old students too help in many different ways. True, often these diverse contributions are just little drops, but don't little drops sometimes add up to make a mighty ocean?

I have seen similar things happen in the case of the Hospitals too. Here we have many doctors who have seen a lot of service elsewhere and have taken voluntary retirement to be in Baba's Hospital in order to serve there full time. This includes people who built up a huge professional reputation before they came here. Many have also come at a young age, consumed with the desire to serve, and unwilling to be tempted by money offered elsewhere. Transformed by Bhagavan Baba, they serve treating the patients as God, and when they do so, love becomes blended with service, or, as Krishna told Arjuna, elevates work to worship. In addition, there are, as in the case of the University, many eminent doctors who regularly come from America, Canada, UK, and Australia to spend their vacations by serving in Baba's Hospitals!

### The Unimaginable Power of Pure Love

Yes, Pure Love is a magical force that makes all sorts of "little drops" to come together in ways unimaginable, producing miracles we cannot dream of. And what Baba has shown consistently over the years, in many ways and in many areas of human activity, is that Pure Love can actually be squeezed out from within each one of us, if only we decide that it shall be. Being totally Selfless, this Love has a power that no wealth can command, for the simple reason that the source of this power is God Himself.

In the *Gita,* Krishna describes how His power is packed into so many of Nature's agents like the Sun and the ocean, for example. Today, humans are trying to tap those sources of energy to meet increased energy demands. However, greater than all that is a power source that God in His infinite mercy has put into each one of us, the Power of Pure and Selfless Love. If only we unlock that source and enable the Love in everyone to be synchronised like a chain of power stations, then more wonders can be achieved than one can dream of. That this is indeed possible, is what Baba has demonstrated.

Let me amplify the last remark, beginning with the example of the laser, which demonstrates the power of coherence in a powerful manner. A laser is just a light source but of a very special kind, in which the atoms that emit the light do so on a very "disciplined" manner. That is to say, all atoms emit light in the same direction and "in step". A more technical way of saying that would be to state that there is both spatial and temporal coherence in the light emitted by a laser. Of course, this does not happen by accident but through a careful design of the source emitting the light. By contrast, the light emitted by an ordinary incandescent bulb or tube light does not have the properties of coherence.

Ensuring coherence of the emitted light takes effort, but it can be very rewarding. For example, these days, carbon dioxide lasers are regularly used in shipyards to cut through steel plates that are five and even ten centimetres thick. In the Lawrence Livermore National Laboratory in America, they have a huge machine built at a cost of a couple of billion dollars I believe, wherein hundreds of powerful laser beams are focussed on a tiny target that is specially made. When all that power is focussed on that target, it gets heated to over a million degrees, the sort of temperatures one gets in the interior of stars; imagine that!

And when the target is heated to that kind of temperature, it explodes like a mini hydrogen bomb, releasing energy via nuclear reactions that go on regularly in the interior of our Sun; such is the power we get by making atoms to act in a coherent manner.

We now take one step back and ask where the idea of the laser came from? From the human brain of course. As Krishna explains, the power of the Mind is a manifestation of one aspect of the power of God. Yes, the human brain is extra-ordinarily powerful, and it is thanks to it that man has landed on the Moon, is able to pick up dirt on Mars and analyse it without actually going there, and send a man-made object out of the solar system deep into space!

What Krishna and Baba call attention to is that one can go up one notch higher than even discovery and creativity, by tapping the **MUCH LARGER** power available in Selfless Love. If that is harnessed, then amazing things are possible. In fact, Baba's mega projects show that such things **CAN** be done. However, when I mention this to people they almost invariably say, "Look, Baba is exceptional; it is one-of-a-kind of example. We cannot follow that. We are ordinary people," and so on.

Unfortunately, it is a great tragedy that so many people insist on lowering their self-esteem! It is not me who is claiming that there is an amazing source of power within each of us, but Krishna and Bhagavan Baba who are saying so! What is more important, Baba has shown again and again, that this power **CAN** be tapped and put to constructive use. Why then is there so much hesitancy to follow His example?

Fortunately, in a few cases at least, the collective Conscience of humanity has been awakened, for example, in connection with matters relating to the environment, bird flu, child labour and abuse, trafficking of women, and so on. In many cases, even the Heads of States and various UN agencies are becoming increasingly involved, all of which are undoubtedly good signs. However, the time has come when humanity needs to go **MUCH** further, and for this, the lead must be taken from the *Gita.* Gandhi tried to do precisely that, by proposing the Trusteeship Model; however, at that time there were not many takers.

The world has moved on since those days, and it is useful to revisit the Trusteeship concept, keeping in mind current needs as well as constraints. In a sense, humanity is trying to do that. However, half-hearted efforts are not enough, and we see this clearly in the case of issues related to climate change, **where we obviously need bolder we need bolder and more emphatic steps.** Mankind has already agreed that Antarctica belongs to no single country; nor does the Moon. Can we take this one step further and say that air, land, oceans and rivers belong, in a sense, to the whole of not only the present generation, but to all generations to come in the future?

Such questions are not receiving the attention they deserve. Take healthcare. Baba's Message is loud and clear. He is essentially asking: "What is the meaning of all the fabulous progress in medical sciences, if it is inaccessible to about 70 percent of humanity? Is it not Society's duty and responsibility to be concerned about the poor and the destitute?" Yes, the question is whether we can [as many tend to] simply dismiss it all as a matter of survival of the fittest, arguing that only those who can pay for the treatment would survive? To create systems that take care of the rich while simply brushing aside the problem of healthcare for the poor is not only foolish but also dangerous. Both the rich and the poor live on the same planet, and thanks to the connectivity we have these days, the sickness of the poor could well spread to such an extent as to threaten the **WHOLE** of the human race. To forsake the poor on various pseudo-economic grounds would be as foolish as a person trying to remain unconcerned, while many organs of his are diseased and sick. The Message that Bhagavan Baba is sending us is that Society simply cannot afford to remain content with Healthcare for just those who can afford today's high rates; to ignore all the rest would be at the peril of all.

Next, consider Education. Almost everywhere, it has become an expensive proposition. They say that by 2050 or so, India would have about 500 million young people–imagine that, half a billion young people! An analyst was asked: "Would this not be a great asset for India at a time when in many countries, the birth rate is falling and the population is aging?" The analyst said in reply: "If these young people are properly educated, it would certainly be a great asset. But if most of these people remain illiterate, then we would be sitting on a time-bomb!" Through His University, Baba is sending us a message that Society simply **CANNOT** afford to reduce education to a marketable commodity.

With every passing day, issues are multiplying; humans today have acquired an **incredible** mastery of Science and Technology, and since these have not always been used in the proper manner, humanity is facing multiple crises. Many years ago, late Victor Weisskopf, a distinguished professor at America's famed university MIT, said, in an address to the American Association for the Advancement of Science: "Knowledge without compassion is inhuman, while compassion without knowledge is ineffective." By knowledge, Weisskopf meant worldly knowledge or more specifically, scientific and technological knowledge. Baba says the same; He observes that knowledge and skill alone are not enough. One must, in addition, have [Spiritual] balance, which alone would lead to insight.

Today, we sorely lack that insight. How else can one explain the fact that countries of the world are spending annually over a **trillion** dollars in defence budget alone, not counting the cost of engaging in actual conflicts, and the post-conflict expenditure associated with rebuilding and rehabilitation? There are over **five thousand** nuclear weapons today–this after many doses of disarmament by the superpowers. Most of the nuclear weapons of today are far deadlier than the bombs dropped over Hiroshima and Nagasaki. What for? Does anyone seriously imagine that any country can drop an atom bomb and getaway with it? Why then, do people want to design new bombs and build supercomputers to test these by simulation [because there is a treaty banning actual tests]?

Hardly anyone is seriously concerned about the fact that while the amount of land available to humans is fixed, and so is the amount of directly usable fresh water, the demand for food is constantly increasing even as the population of the world soars. By the way, let us not assume that agriculture alone requires water. Actually, in the developed world, the *per capita* consumption of water associated with industry and the service sector **exceeds** the demands of agriculture. No wonder, since people constantly want all kinds of new electronic gadgets;

and while they do so, they hardly realise how much water is consumed by the semi-conductor industry in making the chips these gadgets need; nor are people aware what a problem it is to dispose off old TV sets, cell phones and the like, which have dangerous materials in them like lead, beryllium, etc.

### The Individual as a Cosmic Entity

The best way of wrapping all this up is to call attention to a perspective that the *Gita* implies and which I now wish to spell out explicitly. According to me, every single individual, particularly the so-called educated, must constantly be aware of what I call THE FOUR C's. They are:

1. Humans must be conscious of their **Cosmic Origin.**
2. Next, they must always be conscious of their **Cosmic Connections.**
3. They must be ever sensitive to their **Cosmic Responsibilities.**
4. And finally, they must never forget their **Cosmic Destiny.**

Cosmic Origin refers to the fact that we have all come from God [as Krishna Himself declares in the *Gita*], and have, every single one of us without exception, the Divine Genes within us.

Cosmic Connection refers to the Limb Hierarchy mentioned earlier. The *Atma* that pervades the entire Universe and everything that is within it, links us all in a subtle manner, a fact that now finds strong corroboration from Modern Science [recall the quotes of Gary Zukov and Geoffrey Chew].

Cosmic Responsibility calls attention to the fact that no action of ours must ever cause harm to Society in any way or disturb Nature in any manner. It is only such action that would please God. In fact, Baba defines *Dharma* as loving actions that would benefit all, adding that it is such actions that please God most.

Cosmic Destiny is what has been explained by Krishna to Arjuna as the Purpose of Life–from God we all have come, and to God we all should return, the sooner the better!

And now, I wish to draw particular attention to the very last sentence spoken by Krishna in the imaginary dialogue that I have presented. Krishna tells Arjuna, "Don't worry, everything would work out fine. As long as I am by your side, be assured that victory is yours!" This is based on the last *Sloka* in the *Gita* proper, and that *Sloka* is not due to either Krishna or Arjuna. Rather, that is what Sanjaya, the running commentator for Dhritarashtra, offers as a parting comment. Sanjaya says: "Wherever there is Krishna, the Lord of *Yoga,* and wherever there is Partha, the archer, there, be rest assured, lie Victory, Prosperity, Glory and Justice."

There is a special reason why I am making a reference to this. It turns out that shortly before he went on the famous Dandi March by way of launching the Salt Satyagraha [protesting the salt tax levied by the British], Mahatma Gandhi addressed the group of volunteers he was personally leading. He concluded his talk by quoting the last *Sloka* of the *Gita* and said that in real life, Krishna represents the **END** while Arjuna represents the **MEANS.** Gandhi stressed, that in **WHATEVER** we do, both the ends **AND** the means must be pure; only then would we truly succeed. He added that while the policemen deployed to prevent the march might rain blows on them, they the marchers, having sworn by *Ahimsa,* must never resort to violence as a retaliatory measure. Documentary films shot at that time show how the volunteers were attacked by the police with batons, but never replied with violence, despite heavy casualties. These days it is often argued that the end justifies the means. That is not correct; the so-called means and the so-called end, both form a part of a continuous fabric called *Dharma. Dharma* cannot ever be segmented or torn apart to suit one's convenience.

### The Individual, Spirituality and Society

Finally, let me give you a feel for Baba's teachings by presenting a few brief quotes from His innumerable Discourses, quotes that provide an anchor to what I have said in this "Epilogue". I start with one that dispels the popular notion that Spirituality is far, far removed from ordinary and mundane life. Contradicting this view Bhagavan Baba says:

> ***Today, people think that Spirituality has no relation to mundane life and vice versa. This is a big mistake. True Divinity is a combination of Spirituality and social obligations. National unity and social harmony are founded upon Spirituality. It is the Divine that links Spirituality and social existence. The Creator and the Prakriti (Cosmos) are inextricably associated with each other. Hence, God should not be regarded as separate from the Creation. See God in the Cosmos.***
>
> ***- Discourse, 12th Feb 1991***

Next, I wish to draw attention to the fact that Spirituality is all about relating our actions to helping humanity in every possible way and, in the process, becoming aware of the Divine Nature of the Spirit within us. The quote below stresses what I earlier referred to as our Cosmic Responsibility. Concerning this Bhagavan Baba says:

> ***There are questions raised: Of what relation is Society and social ties with the Spirit and its glory? Of what relation is the Spirit with Society's tangles and trickeries? Such questions arise from erring minds. Spiritual endeavour must aim at individual illumination, social betterment and the Divinization of the human community. This is extremely urgent and essential. Through service to Society, the Divinity inherent in man can blossom more quickly, more widely, more fragrantly. Presently you recognize the world, but, not God who is immanent in it! So too, you see the individual but, not the corpus that is immanent in Society.***
>
> ***- Discourse, October 1971***

Notice the stress on seeing God in Society. Baba often reminds His students that this is indeed what the Vedic hymn *Purusha Sukhtam* conveys, adding, "Service to man, is service to God."

All of us yearn for peace but how many realize that peace is not the mere absence of conflict, and that we cannot enjoy true peace unless there is peace and harmony in the entire neighbourhood, and indeed in the whole world? That peace has to start first with peace within, which manifests when Love from the Heart flows outwards in thoughts, words and deeds, seeing God everywhere. Commenting on this, Bhagavan Baba says:

> ***Your peace and happiness are linked with the world's peace and happiness. Any act of hatred or violence committed by you will pollute the atmosphere of the world. Adore any living being, and the adoration reaches God, for He is in every being. Insult any living being, and the insult too reaches God. So, expand love towards all, everywhere.***
>
> ***- Discourse, August 15, 1985***

The Cosmic Responsibility that I referred to does not make any sense unless there is first a spirit of sacrifice. The word "sacrifice" often carries an unpleasant connotation, implying pain, denial, etc. However, for the person deeply involved, it represents instead, the joy of giving. Sacrifice is the undercurrent of all of Baba's teachings, and that is so because it is also the undercurrent of the *Vedas* and the *Gita.* Again and again, Baba tells His students: "You are what you are because of Society; you therefore owe a debt to Society. When you go out, your main aim must be to serve Society in every way you can." Amazingly, Bill Gates too has often stressed the debt we owe to Society. In fact, Andrew Carnegie, Warren Buffet and many others also have stressed the same. Baba, however, raises the discussion to a much higher plane and says:

> ***It is only when the individual is prepared to sacrifice his selfish desires and toil for the***

***welfare of Society that the Nation will prosper. Then only would the world have peace. That is why the Vedas proclaim that man can have peace only when he renounces selfish desires. The Vedas express disapproval of persons who accumulate wealth and who are ever immersed in activities that can add to their physical comfort. The man who gives, receives even while he gives, more than what he gives.***

***- Discourse, March 29, 1979***

This quote explains the merit and the practical benefit we receive from "sacrifice"; it is when we "sacrifice" and bring joy to others that we find real peace within us. Once we are filled with peace, that peace would unquestionably make its impact outside, even as fragrance flows from a flower, bringing a nice feeling to all who are able to catch that fragrance. Incidentally, this is the reason why people flock to have the *Darshan* of holy men, and go to serene places. Something there passes on to the devotees, filling them also with peace. There is an important, crucial, and practical point to be noted here. These days, there is a feeling that peace, especially where there is a major conflict, would come only through discussions, negotiations, bargaining, etc. That is the bureaucratic view, and does have some utility that cannot be denied. However, as Gandhi showed many a time, it is when a messenger filled with peace, actually goes to the scene of violence and fury, that the seeds of peace are truly sown.

And now, I offer two quotes that have great relevance to the issue of Trusteeship that I argued for earlier. In the first quote,

Baba reminds us that every single individual has a stake in what happens to the world. We all live in the world, and faced as we are with many huge problems, we cannot expect to be insulated from what happens to the world. Clearly, the world has to be put back on the rails, and this is too important a task to be left solely to politicians, statesmen and diplomats, including those in the various units of the UN. True, all these people do have their own roles to play. However, as the primary stakeholders, it is **WE** who have the basic responsibility of taking care of, and the fixing of problems. Calling attention to this, Bhagavan Baba says:

> ***The world has to be brought back to the rails. Only love and peace can achieve this. Fill your thoughts, speech and actions with love, truth and peace, and engage yourselves in service activity. We aspire for peace and comfort all the time, but where can we find it? Is it to be found in the material world around us? Experience shows that the peace or happiness got from external objects is not enduring. It is like a mirage, which cannot quench the thirst of the deluded animal that runs towards it. The real source of peace is within every individual and it is this inner peace that can confer real joy.***
>
> ***- Discourse, December 9, 1985***

I trust this quote brings to your mind Krishna telling Arjuna that happiness does not reside in objects of the external world but is a state of being.

More now about Trusteeship. While discoursing on this

concept, Gandhi examines the merit of the socialist ideology that earlier inspired many economists and intellectuals, leading even to many countries adopting what was called the socialist model. Gandhi says that all these were experiments in trying to achieve "arithmetic equality". History has demonstrated that while this approach to the removal of inequity does have merit as also great attraction, in the long run it invariably fails, the collapse of the erstwhile Soviet Union being perhaps the classic example. Interestingly, China, which until a few decades ago was a rigid adherent to the Communist doctrine, has now switched to [state-sponsored] Capitalism that has not only brought a return to inequity, but has in fact exacerbated it. Gandhi wanted instead what he called Moral Socialism, which is nothing but the Trusteeship model that I alluded to earlier. Basically, the emphasis shifts from a "mechanical" equal distribution of wealth to feeling one in Spirit with everyone, and sharing as well as caring for all. Commenting on this, Bhagavan Baba says:

> ***There has been talk of achieving equality in Society. The equal distribution of wealth through socialism is declared as the ideal, but is it possible to bring about such equality? Even if material wealth is distributed equally, can you ensure equality in desires and aspirations? You must look beyond material things to the Supreme Being who is the provider of all things. When you recognize the One as present in all beings, and respect everyone as a manifestation of the Divine, you will achieve equality in the true sense of the term.***
>
> ***- Discourse, December 11, 1985***

The half a dozen quotes I have offered do not represent even the tip of the "iceberg" of Swami's teachings. Rather, they represent just a typical sample, meant to indicate that Bhagavan Baba has commented in detail on every aspect of life, both at the individual as well as at the societal level. Hints for further reading are offered at the end, but in the meantime, before I bring this to a close, there are a few comments I would like to make.

1. Greed is infectious, and collective greed is like the small-pox virus, with the deadly ability to spread rapidly. Once the virus of greed spreads and produces extensive infection, tension quickly builds up leading to conflicts of various kinds.

2. In any conflict, there are basically two parties, one which has the "upper hand" and the other the "lower hand". Usually, the side that is dominant is smaller in terms of absolute numbers, but makes up for it with military might, financial clout, technological superiority, industrial muscle, and the like. The other side is usually a disjointed collection of ill-prepared, ill-organised, and ill-trained people, with not much resources of any kind. However, often their number is large, and driven by a fierce anger against the injustices meted out, they fight back, in ways that the other party is not accustomed to.

3. Thus prolonged conflicts result, and right now there are many such raging in different parts of the world, all the way from the Philippines to Columbia, with any number of countries in between, in both Asia and Africa. Almost everywhere it is lose-lose situation with both sides losing, one side losing more in terms of human lives and the other side losing more in terms of social cost; the crisis in the Middle East

that has been going on for sixty years is a very good example.

4. There is only one way to end all such deadlocks, which is for the side having the "upper hand" to show some **real** magnanimity, and "bend down" to make a few generous concessions to the demands of the opposite side. Currently, "experts" view this as caving in and surrendering. This view, which is based entirely on ego, finds acceptance, because individuals, communities and even nations too are chained to the same ego. Collective ego is born out of individual ego, which is why every single individual must strive independently to vanquish the ego within. If the ice has to be broken and thaw must set in, then one must move from the "ego perspective" to a different perspective where one sees the other person also as a child of God, and thus, an extension of oneself.

5. It is not as if there are no historical examples of such an approach; in fact, conciliatory approaches have been tried many times, and with success too. However, when one is in the grip of a mindset created by the forces of fear and selfishness, one easily tends to forget the good lessons of history. In this context, it is very useful to make a careful study of how Nelson Mandela avoided a blood bath in South Africa, when apartheid came to an end.

What I have tried to show in this book is that magnanimity, compassion, generosity, the idea of sharing and caring are not alien to basic human nature. On the contrary, they are the very essence of human nature, and for a good reason, which is that every little bit of goodness within us originates from the Divine Spark within.

I have met many scholars belonging to different faiths, all of whom told me that in the ultimate analysis, every conflict originates in the Mind of the individual human being, World War II being the classic example. The war itself involved so many countries and millions of soldiers, causing the death eventually of about twenty million people. But they all were triggered because one man's Mind became a prisoner to the deadliest enemies of man.

Stated differently, the Mahabharatha War, at the beginning of which Krishna spoke to and advised Arjuna, is in a manner constantly waging within each one of us all the time, with the Mind being pulled one way by the senses and the *Atma* pulling the Mind the other way, in order to save it. In this war, the Mind is like the ordinary soldier. The soldier named Arjuna, aligned himself with Krishna or the *Atma;* that is why he ultimately emerged victorious. The soldier named Duryodhana, aligned himself with people who had become slaves to the enemies of man, namely greed, selfishness, etc. That is why Duryodhana eventually lost everything including his life, which sends us a message.

The war that is waging inside each of us has to be won by us as individuals; and this is where the individual *sadhana* or Spiritual cleansing [read Mind and sense control] becomes extremely important. When individuals, who have at least to some extent, contained the destabilising forces within, get together, the collective and coherent aspects begin to manifest in the world outside, and that is how we can put the world back on its rails.

There is a passage in the Bible that says:

*For we are strangers before Thee, and sojourners, as were our fathers. Our days on the earth are as a shadow, and there is none abiding.*

The second line in the above is what I wish to focus on, for it reminds us that our existence here on earth is transient. The *Gita* teaches us how to pack that fleeting existence with meaning and purpose by focussing on Eternity. In brief, it boils down to aligning our entire life to God, using a Moral Compass.

The point was made beautifully during the American Civil War by President Abraham Lincoln. A Minister from the North, while visiting Lincoln in the White House, said how glad he was that God was on the Union's side [being led by Lincoln]. Lincoln corrected the Minister by saying, "Sir, my concern is not whether God is on our side; my greatest concern is to be on God's side." I believe the *Gita* teaches us all how to go through life being on God's side all the time. Adapting one of Lincoln's famous statement, I think the best description of the *Gita* is that it is of the Heart, from the Heart and to the Heart; that is to say, the Message is from God, to humans who are embodiments of God, and intended to raise them to the level of God.

Before signing off, let me thank you for being with me. I do hope that you have been benefited by what I have offered, and feel the urge to know more. To help with and assist in that process, I present below some leads by way of suggestions for further reading as also media exploration that hopefully would complement the understanding gained from this book.

*SAMASTHA LOKHAA SUKHINO BHAVANTU!*

*May every being in all the worlds be happy!*

**Suggestions for further reading and exploration**

There are many books available, but of these, the following two would be good to start with, in the present context.

1. ***Conversations with Bhagavan Sri Sathya Sai Baba,*** by Dr. John S. Hislop, available at the Publications Division of the Sri Sathya Sai Sadhana Trust, Prasanthi Nilayam.

2. ***Bhagavad Gita[Parts I and II]***. This is a compilation of discourses delivered by Bhagavan Baba on the Bhagavad Gita. The book also is published by the Publications Division of the Sri Sathya Sai Sadhana Trust, Prasanthi Nilayam.

In addition, the reader is invited to browse through the on-line journal ***Heart 2 Heart***. This journal is published by Radio Sai, a 24/7 radio channel available on WorldSpace and internet (www.radiosai.org).

The e-journal referred to is a treasure chest of inspiring articles covering various facets of Baba's life, teachings and missions, some of which have been briefly referred to in this book.

For access to the e-journal ***Heart 2 Heart*** please visit www.h2hsai.org

# GLOSSARY

Note: Presented here is a glossary of Sanskrit words that appear in the text. In the text, the uppercase is used for the first alphabet of the words with a Spiritual connotation (like *Atma*) or having a link to a Divine attribute (like *Dharma*). In all other cases (like in the word *karma*, for example), the lower case has been used.

| | |
|---|---|
| *Adharma* | opposite of *Dharma*; unrighteousness. |
| *Ahamkara* | ego |
| *Ahimsa* | non-violence |
| *Ajnana* | Spiritual ignorance |
| *Ananda* | Supreme Bliss |
| *Atma* | God, Absolute Reality, Universal Self |
| *Atma Bhavam* | feeling one with the *Atma* |
| *Atma Dharma* | Righteous action in full accord with the *Atma* |
| *Atma Jnana* | Supreme Wisdom |
| *Atma Vidya* | Knowledge of the Supreme Self |
| *Atmaabhimaanam* | love for the *Atma* |
| *Avatar* | an incarnation of the Formless God |
| | |
| *Bhagavat Preethyartham* | for the pleasure of the Lord |
| *Bhakti* | devotion to the Lord |
| *Yoga* | becoming one with God through devotion |
| *Brahman* | Supreme Lord |

| | |
|---|---|
| *Niraakara* | God in the Formless Aspect |
| *Saakara* | God with Form |
| *Buddhi* | faculty of Spiritual Discrimination |
| | |
| *Daya* | Compassion |
| *Dehaabhimaanam* | body-consciousness |
| *Deva* | demi-god, a deity who resides in heaven |
| *Dharma* | Righteousness |
| | |
| *Gayathri* | a prayer addressed to the Universal Mother |
| *Guna* | intrinsic behavioural trait |
| *Guru* | Spiritual teacher |
| | |
| *Himsa* | violence |
| | |
| *Janma* | a birth |
| *Jiva* | living being |
| *Jivatma* | individual Soul |
| *Jnana* | Supreme Wisdom |
| *Jnanendriya* | faculty of cognition |
| *Jnani* | a Realised Soul |
| | |
| *Kama* | desire |
| *Karma* | action |
| *Karma Phala* | fruit of action |
| *Karma Phala Tyagam* | giving up the claim to fruit of action |

| | |
|---|---|
| *Karma Yoga* | becoming one with God through righteous action |
| *Karmendriya* | faculty of sense perception |
| *Karuna* | Kindness |
| *Krishnaarpanam* | offering to Krishna |
| *Krodha* | anger |
| *Kshama* | Forbearance |
| | |
| *Leela* | a play of the Lord |
| *Janma* | the *Avatar's* life as a part of the overall Divine Drama |
| *Lobha* | greed |
| | |
| *Madha* | pridc |
| *Mamakara* | sense of mine |
| *Manthra* | a scriptural hymn |
| *Matsarya* | jealousy |
| *Medha Shakti* | worldly intelligence |
| *Moha* | infatuation, attachment |
| | |
| *Naamasmarana* | chanting the Name of the Lord |
| | |
| *Paramatma* | Universal Self |
| *Parameshti* | God |
| *Praana Shakti* | life force |
| *Prakriti* | Nature |
| *Prema* | Divine Love |
| *Punyam* | merit earned through righteous action |

| | |
|---|---|
| *Purusha Sukhtam* | a particular Vedic prayer, in praise of the Omnipresent God |
| *Sadguru* | the *Guru* of *Gurus*, i.e., God |
| *Samashti* | Society |
| *Sankalpa* | resolution |
| *Sathya* | Truth |
| *Shanti* | Peace |
| *Srishti* | Creation |
| *Trikaranasuddhi* | purity of thought, word and deed |
| *Upanishad* | a text of Vedantic philosophy |
| *Veda* | ancient scripture, compiled from Divine revelations |
| *Vyashti* | individual |
| *Yajna* | a Vedic ritual, usually for propitiating a particular deity |
| *Rajasuya* | a particular type of *Yajna* |
| *Yoga* | best understood as a pathway to God |
| *Yoga Vasishtam* | this is the name of the teaching imparted by Sage Vasishta to Prince Rama during the latter's adolescence |